LISTENING, LEARNING
AND LEADING

LISTENING, LEARNING AND LEADING:
The impact of Catholic identity and mission

Connor Court Publishing
Ballarat

Connor Court Publishing Pty Ltd 2014

Copyright © Catholic Social Services Victoria 2014

ALL RIGHTS RESERVED. This book contains material protected under International and Federal Copyright Laws and Treaties. Any unauthorised reprint or use of this material is prohibited. No part of this book may be reproduced or transmitted in any form or by any means, electronic or mechanical, including photocopying, recording, or by any information storage and retrieval system without express written permission from the publisher.

PO Box 224W
Ballarat VIC 3350
sales@connorcourt.com
www.connorcourt.com

ISBN: 9781925138177 (pbk.)

Cover and title page graphic designs by Rita Terunawidjaja (Catholic Communications)

'Poem for Marie' (p. 152) is taken from *Open Ground* by Seamus Heaney, published by Faber & Faber

Printed in Australia

CONTENTS

Foreword: Communication and the Catholic Identity
Tim Fischer   vii

Introduction
Learning and Leading: The Impact of Catholic Identity and Mission
Gabrielle McMullen and John Warhurst   1

Part One: General Perspectives

1 The Heart of the Matter
Margaret Mary Flynn ibvm   17

2 Called to Lead: Leadership to Make Mission a Reality
Chris Lowney   33

3 Sharing the Mission with the Whole Organisation
Julie Edwards   47

4 Catholics' Radical Alternative
Frank Brennan SJ   63

Part Two: Specific Questions

5 Are We There Yet? – Engagement with Aboriginal Communities
Vicki Clark and Peter Hudson   77

6 At the Crossroads: The Challenges of Child Sexual Abuse to Mission and Identity
Jenny Glare   87

7 Engaging, Exploring and Enabling: Lessons in Executive Leadership from the Gospel of John
Julie Morgan   103

8 Position Vacant/Position Filled – Mission Flourishing!
Getting Recruitment and Induction Right
David Beaver and Peter Hudson   111

9 The Changing Face of the Catholic Community in Australia:
Challenges for Catholic Social Service Organisations
Robert Dixon   123

Part Three: Personal Reflections

10 Greatly Amused: Mary MacKillop and the One Habit of a
Highly Effective Leader
Michael McGirr   143

11 Mission Shapes Identity
Andrew Hamilton SJ   153

12 Listening, Learning and Leading – A Continuing Dialogue:
Inspiring Us to be Christ in the World Today
Denis Fitzgerald   165

Contributor Details   181

Foreword
Communication and the Catholic Identity

Tim Fischer

Leadership does not always come naturally, even to admirals and generals let alone bishops and cardinals. Yet in the earliest of Christian times, the Apostolic Fathers, despite facing difficulties and resistance from the world of that time, gave outstanding examples of leadership from "Jerusalem to Illyricum". Illyricum was the Roman province embracing modern Albania, Croatia and Slovenia and St Paul writing to the Romans (*Romans* 15:19) said he had preached the Gospel there, and planned to go even further afield, and he did.

All the Apostles and other early Church leaders, often after initial stumbles, gave outstanding examples of leadership. This helped establish leadership templates, and none were more impressive than those created by St Paul and St Peter. They had to adapt the good news of the Gospel without compromising and adopting the contemporary and dominant Graeco-Roman values. This was never easy.

Malta is not known for an immediate embrace of the many strangers and forces that have washed up on its shores over the centuries, but the Maltese quickly came under the spell of St Paul, converting to Christianity which remains the dominant religion to this day, two thousand years on. St Paul had survived a shipwreck on the shores of Malta whilst en route to Rome but did not waste time on self-pity but rather seized the suddenly arising opportunity.

In all of the business of getting the message across, which is the essential ingredient of mission and leadership, there must be a fundamental ability to communicate. I have often said good leadership is first and thrice about communication, communication, communication as well as all other attributes.

Post Vatican Council II, the Roman Catholic Church made some bold steps to enhance communication with its followers and beyond, commencing with the symbolic turning around of the altars so priests faced their congregation. Momentum has waxed and waned since, due in part to the buffeting caused by the ever-shrill drumbeats of atheism and secularism throughout our society.

As referred to in this publication, St Mary MacKillop was a 'leader extraordinaire', contributing in two centuries of great change and overcoming enormous hurdles without ever walking away from her faith and fundamental loyalties. St Mary made it across the unsafe Tasman Sea many times as well as right through to Rome, Britain, France, Scotland and even Ireland. Her ability to communicate in words and her writings was legendary and led directly to the formation of the Sisters of St Joseph religious order and her excellent leadership of same.

So as we enjoy and absorb the key messages, the key contents, of all that follows in this publication we need to think also about how to convey the messages and the mission further. In this regard there are many simple practical steps, including being presentable, polite, precise, punctual but above all else positive and passionate.

It has to be said that stating a case without energy, without discerning effort and without clarity is a waste of time. Indeed, stating a case without the passion that comes from a strong faith conviction, without sensitivity, empathy, discernment and respectful listening, will reap little fruit, if any. Above all else clarity is an absolute requirement.

In this regard, mixed signals from various echelons of the Church in Rome and throughout many levels within various Bishops' conferences can be very confusing for well-intentioned laypeople trying to follow their faith loyally. To put it bluntly, do the declarations of Vatican Council II stand or are they to be gradually eroded away?

Post Vatican Council II, no Pope has formally done other than support the declarations of Pope Paul VI. But at times mixed messages have emerged, mixed signals have been given out. It is as if somehow Vatican Council II was optional, it could somehow be ignored or bypassed or even reversed by prelates and laypersons alike.

This is why the work of Catholic Social Services Victoria (CSSV) is so vital and, through various key seminars and conferences, much leadership is provided and disseminated. This is especially so with the CSSV's conference of 8-9 October 2013 entitled *Listening, Learning and Leading: The impact of Catholic identity and mission on what we do and how we do it*, which inspired this book.

The publication does seek to engage, inspire, challenge and more, and it does so under the guidance of various key presenters whose papers are contained herein. As such it happily marches alongside the spirit of renewal and revamping flowing from the Holy Father, Pope Francis, who is delivering so much and so rapidly in his first dynamic year in office.

As you study the papers that follow, as each of us tries to take up the cudgels for a better and Christian-oriented society, we do so helped by both the work of CSSV and the bold leadership of the 266th occupant of the Throne of St Peter as the first Southern Hemisphere, first Argentinian, first Jesuit Holy Father, resident downstairs at the hotel Santa Marta in Vatican City – namely Pope Francis.

Introduction
Learning and Leading:
The Impact of Catholic Identity and Mission

Gabrielle McMullen and John Warhurst

Catholic organisations across Australia are actively engaged in the mission of the Church, through ministries to the community in social services, health and education. In his first encyclical, *Deus Caritas Est*, Pope Benedict XVI emphasises the significance of these ministries:

> The Church's deepest nature is expressed in her three-fold responsibility: of proclaiming the word of God (*kerygmamartyria*), celebrating the sacraments (*leitourgia*), and exercising the ministry of charity (*diakonia*). These duties presuppose each other and are inseparable. For the Church, charity is not a kind of welfare activity which could equally well be left to others, but is a part of her nature, an indispensable expression of her very being.[1]

The relationship of these ministries to the broader Church, and the challenges and opportunities that this presents for those associated with them, are important matters, that will be influential in determining the future of these services, and the extent to which they can continue to contribute to the development of our society.

Catholic Social Services Victoria's (CSSV) conference of 8-9 October 2013 entitled *Listening, Learning and Leading: The impact of*

---

1 Pope Benedict XVI, Encyclical Letter, *Deus Caritas Est*, 2005, section 25; accessed on 7 November 2013 at vatican.va.

Catholic identity and mission on what we do and how we do it, which provided the impetus for this book, sought to "engage, inspire, challenge and resource around leadership for Catholic identity and mission". The feedback would suggest that the conference achieved its stated aims and in the longer term, through the work of the Spirit and the passionate and compassionate service of conference participants, the conference's 'ripple effect' will potentially influence Catholic ministries in a sustained and enlivening manner. This collation of papers from the conference seeks to foster that endeavour and open up to a wider audience the insights of practitioners, theologians and commentators offered at the conference.

* * * *

During their pontificates, Popes John Paul II and Benedict XVI gave particular impetus to Catholic agencies across the globe reviewing the nature of their ministry and explicitly strengthening their Catholic identity and mission. The secularisation of the wider society and the "culture of relativism" identified by Pope Benedict XVI have driven the critical need to engage with Catholic identity and mission. Pope Francis, in turn, has emphasised the importance of coherence between personal and agency identity so that the witness of staff reflects the essence of a Catholic agency.

Fifty years after the Second Vatican Council, we are seeing manifestly the fulfilment of its call for greater lay participation in the Church. In particular, Catholic social services, health and education have undergone, or are undergoing, the transition from priests and religious founding and conducting such agencies to their lay leadership and staffing.

For the flourishing of this new era of lay participation in the Church, we need to be profoundly conscious of the impact that this change can have on Catholic identity, for better or worse. Of critical importance is the formation of lay leaders, and of those who would be leaders, to animate Christ's mission in the modern world through their ministry of the Church.

In response to these "signs of the times",[2] CSSV has provided leadership both in engagement with Catholic identity and mission and in providing induction and formation for leaders and staff of its member agencies. For example, in 2009 under the auspices of Bishop Christopher Prowse, the then Episcopal Vicar for Justice and Social Services, CSSV conducted three seminars on strengthening Catholic identity in health, welfare and education agencies in the Archdiocese of Melbourne.

These forums offered leaders and experts engaged in these fields of the Church's mission of service a theological underpinning for their ministry as they shared views and experience of practice.[3] Other Church agencies have been similarly exploring Catholic identity and mission – for example, Australian Catholic University hosted four cross-sectoral colloquia on identity and mission in Church-based organisations in 2007-2010.[4]

What do we Mean by Catholic Identity and Mission?

During his time on earth Jesus was on a mission from his Father. In our ministries of social services, health and education, we continue his mission, witnessing to the love of God. Thus, by mission

---

2   Pope John XXIII, Encyclical, *Pacem in Terris*, 1963, section 126; accessed on 26 January 2014 at vatican.va.
3   Denis Fitzgerald, *Kairos Catholic Journal*, 2009, 20(4), pp. 8-9; 2009, 20(5), pp. 10-12; 2009, 20(6), pp. 8-9; accessed on 6 February 2014 at cam.org.au/Kairos.
4   The proceedings of the 2007 colloquium were subsequently published: Neil Ormerod (ed.), *Identity and Mission in Catholic Agencies*, St Pauls Publications, Strathfield, NSW, 2008.

we mean the mission of Jesus Christ. For Catholic agencies, that is a particular work or works undertaken as a ministry of the Church or, in the words of Pope Benedict cited above, "exercising the ministry of charity ... an indispensable expression of her very being". Significantly, agency "implies some notion of identity"[5] and Bishop Michael Putney of Townsville has highlighted that "the question of Catholic identity is a far more complex and profound question than sometimes is realized".[6]

Dr Gerry Arbuckle SM in *Crafting Catholic Identity in Postmodern Australia* presents a "general definition of Catholic identity in the healing ministries", namely:

> It is the ongoing process of the healing mission of Jesus Christ-engaging-with-the-internal-and-external-context of each healthcare facility, according to the Roman Catholic tradition.[7]

Similarly, Catholic social services and education, through consideration of their internal and external environments, arrive at a concept of their Catholic identity, specific for the time and the place, while consistent with their nature as a ministry of the Church. Arbuckle highlights that "there are many ways of identifying what 'Catholic' means" and prefers the concept of Catholic identities.[8]

Thus, at the heart of Catholic identity is the mission of Jesus

---

5   Frank Quinlan, ibid., pp. 41-42, "Common Challenges for Health, Education and Social Services".
6   Michael Putney, ibid., p. 15, "Catholic Identity and Mission".
7   Gerald A. Arbuckle, *Crafting Catholic Identity in Postmodern Australia*, Catholic Health Australia, Canberra, 2007, pp. 12-13.
8   Gerald A. Arbuckle, *Catholic Identity or Identities? Refounding Ministries in Chaotic Times*, Liturgical Press, Collegeville MN, 2013, p. xvii. For the exploration of 'Catholic identities', see also in this book Bob Dixon's paper "The Changing Face of the Catholic Community in Australia: Challenges for Catholic Social Service Organisations".

Christ, and those who work in Catholic ministries represent Christ's presence to those whom they serve in social service agencies, hospitals, hospices, aged care facilities and schools.

Achieving the Right Balance

The critical balance between identity and mission represents a tension for Catholic ministries. If the focus is too narrowly on Catholic identity, a Catholic agency may be seen as exclusive and its mission of witnessing to the love of God will be compromised. On the other hand, an over-emphasis on mission risks reducing the agency to a "generalised form of humanism ... and it [then] loses its specific contribution to the transformation of the world".[9]

Remaining Christ-focused is vital to realising this balance – what is required of those in Catholic ministries was articulated incisively by then Bishop Tim Costelloe SDB in his address at the above-mentioned 2009 CSSV seminars:

> ... if Catholic identity is about witnessing to the compassion, mercy and selflessness of Christ, about being the living sign of Christ's ongoing presence in our world, and it certainly is, then if we wish to strengthen our Catholic identity, we have to strengthen the quality, genuineness and inclusiveness of our outreach to all those who seek the enhancement of their lives though our ministry and presence.[10]

---

9   Neil Ormerod, "Identity and Mission in Catholic Organisations", *The Australasian Catholic Record*, 2010, 87(4), p. 439.
10 Timothy Costelloe, "The Theoretical Underpinnings of Catholic Identity – A Theological Perspective", paper presented at the *Strengthening Catholic Identity in Health, Welfare and Education Agencies* seminar of 3 March 2009, Thomas Carr Centre, East Melbourne, p. 3.

Constant Re-engagement with Catholic Identity and Mission

The ongoing engagement of CSSV with Catholic identity and mission acknowledges that they are never static – there must be constant re-engagement with identity and mission as circumstances change, and this is a time of significant change for social services, health and education, the Church and wider society. Ormerod notes that "identity will change over time as the Church is transformed by its fidelity to its mission"[11] and Ranson highlights that identity "is not something 'possessed', but rather a dimension that is both constant and unfolding".[12] Each Catholic agency will craft its "Catholic identity in ways that specifically fit its local internal and external environments" and this is:

> ... a creative process that is an ongoing, never-ending challenge as the conditions around us change ... the process is not an academic exercise by a few theological experts, but a process in which people in creating Catholic identity are themselves at the same time transforming both their lives and the world around them.[13]

In its 2013 conference and ongoing initiatives addressing Catholic identity and mission, CSSV is making an important and valued contribution to re-engagement in the Australian context.

---

11 Ormerod, Neil, op. cit., "Identity and Mission in Catholic Organisations", p. 432.
12 David Ranson, "Institutions Shaped by Catholic Identity in a Pluralist and Secular Context", paper presented to the Catholic Social Services Australia (NSW/ACT Branch) Conference, Canberra, 19 November 2007, pp. 1-8; accessed on 22 April 2011 at centacare-canberra.org/; David Ranson, "A Service Shaped by Catholic Identity" in Ormerod, Neil, op. cit., *Identity and Mission in Catholic Agencies*, pp. 83-99.
13 Arbuckle, Gerald A., op. cit., *Crafting Catholic Identity in Postmodern Australia*, p. 27.

Mission as the "Senior Partner"

For Catholic ministries operating in the contemporary environment, there are often tensions between sustaining Catholic identity and viability, between fulfilling the mission, in particular service of the disadvantaged and marginalised, and budget imperatives, whereby "the mission is to be the senior partner driving or permeating *all* decisions in the business side".[14]

Critically, for Catholic ministries to achieve their 'full identity' they must achieve both a high standard of service and unequivocal Catholicity. Thus, business implies excellence rather than just viability. Further, leadership of Catholic ministries, besides professionalism, calls for a sense of mission and "accepting, and being transformed by, the values and truths of Catholic identity".[15]

Across Catholic ministries we need ongoing "examination of conscience" in relation to their Catholic identity to ensure that we progress from mission statements to resulting actions and then ultimately to internalised Catholic identity.[16]

This CSSV conference, *Listening, Learning and Leading: The impact of Catholic identity and mission on what we do and how we do it*, provided many examples of good processes in this regard and of the mission of Christ flourishing in Catholic ministries.

This Book

The conference papers assembled in this book contribute in different ways to our understanding of mission and identity in Catholic social

---

14 Ibid., pp. 7 and 84.
15 Ibid., p. 83.
16 Kami Timm, "An Examination of Conscience: The Catholic Identity of Catholic Health Care", *Health Progress*, 2012, 93(1), pp. 7-11; accessed on 23 September 2012 at chausa.org.

service agencies. They are organised into three parts according to their scope and purpose: general perspectives, specific questions and personal reflections.

Explicitly and implicitly this conversation is inspired by the example and teaching of Pope Francis in his first year in office and what we know of his life prior to his election. Pope Francis hovered over this conference and inspired its participants.

For Chris Lowney, author of *Pope Francis: Why He Leads the Way He Leads*, the inspiration comes both from Francis' previous life as a Jesuit leader and his teaching since becoming Pope. As a Jesuit leader, Jorge Bergoglio urges us to get our feet dusty in the world around us, and as Pope he wants the Church to be an inclusive home for all, not just for a select, privileged few.

Also running as a major theme through a number of the papers, especially those by Julie Edwards, Chris Lowney and Frank Brennan SJ, are the lessons of Ignatian spirituality as expressed by Jesuits and their companions living in the particular spirit of St Ignatius of Loyola.

Part One – General Perspectives

Margaret Mary Flynn IBVM's chapter is both aspirational and firmly practical. Jesus is the best model of Catholic mission and identity. The heart of the matter is to be found in "new ways of relating to those who are most vulnerable". Those who see us in our ministries should increasingly 'glimpse' God. We should reach out, by way of example, to Aboriginal mothers or to farming families and, in each case, we should be reaching out to those with whom we are working rather than expecting them to come to us.

Julie Edwards, too, identifies ways in which the Gospel challenge to us individually can be taken up by organisations. In her case, Jesuit Social Services have some 200 staff and 200 volunteers. For her our mission "will be evident in things like how we treat each other, our commitment to those most in need, how we conduct our meetings, how we manage our resources". What we profess must be matched by our actions. Jesuit Social Services draws on the story and spirituality of St Ignatius, a pilgrim, to shape the way the agency works. His values include the centrality of relationship and being in solidarity with the poor and marginalised. The ultimate aim is a just society and the emphasis is always on the human spirit and the dignity of every person. She uses the powerful image of a tree to bring pastoral and business practices together. The mission is the roots of the tree, without which the organisation cannot prosper. The roots are the life force. Without mission the organisation is like a tree without roots.

Chris Lowney makes the point that leadership is a profoundly spiritual idea. Like Isaiah the path to leadership is to know ourselves well, including our weaknesses and our faults. He identifies two central traits in a spirituality of leadership: a sense of purpose greater than self, which he calls heroism, and a deep self-awareness and a habit of reflection. Heroism applies to anyone, anywhere in the organisation. It is not restricted to those in high office. Self-awareness must be worked at and Lowney offers the Ignatian tool of a daily regimen of two 'mental pit stops'. At these times we remind ourselves of what we have to be grateful for, what our larger goals are and what the last few hours have taught us. Following Pope Francis, he calls on us to get our shoes dusty, start finding new paths, live heroically and embrace our leadership vocation.

Catholic Social Teaching (CST) must underpin our Catholic mission and identity. For Frank Brennan SJ our CST language must always be prophetic, pedagogical and practical, reflected in our words, actions and structures. Brennan takes us into the world where faith intersects with politics and his examples are drawn from the contested issues of asylum seekers and refugees, ones addressed with compassion by Pope Francis, and which were a focus in the 2013 Australian federal election.

Part Two – Specific Questions

Mission and identity must involve building a stronger collaborative relationship with our Aboriginal and Torres Strait Islander brothers and sisters through the systematic implantation of the principles of Catholic Social Teaching. For this task Vicki Clark with Peter Hudson introduce also the principles of the landmark Aboriginal Cultural Competence Framework. Negative stereotypes of Aboriginal and Torres Strait Islander peoples must be challenged at every opportunity and appropriate protocols must be in place in every Catholic social services agency. Agencies must know the communities with which they are working. Clark and Hudson provide examples of agencies with good practices. As they say, it is about being faithful to the Gospel values of justice, equity and love of neighbour. This means not just words but a commitment to building a better world for everyone.

The crime of child sexual abuse is mentioned in several chapters. Jenny Glare addresses the challenge for mission and identity of such abuse within the Church.

Julie Morgan engages with the Gospel of John as she returns the conversation to learning lessons of leadership. Jesus models leadership in his actions and introduces the notion that the person who wants to be a leader must first be a servant. One such leadership encounter occurs in the conversation between Jesus and the woman at the well.

The contemporary leader should engage with people as they develop strategies for deep learning where the head, the heart and the spirit grow and expand.

David Beaver with Peter Hudson writes about the importance of recruitment and induction of leaders and all staff for an agency in realising its mission and identity. Centacare Ballarat commits itself to promoting and defending human rights, relying on the moralities of social justice, fairness, love and responsibility. In order to communicate these moralities to a diverse staff and to a secular public it also re-articulates its Catholic identity by reflecting on the relationship between Catholic Social Teaching and the more widely known Universal Declaration of Human Rights.

To address mission and identity we must know both our organisation's staff and our clients. Bob Dixon analyses the changing face of the Catholic community within which the search for identity and the challenge of mission take place. The demography of Australian Catholics is being altered by the character of Catholic immigration and by changing beliefs and practices. One of the most striking characteristics is ethnic diversity. The Australian Church owes much to its immigrants, especially those from non-English speaking countries. Dixon also identifies challenges for social service agencies, including declining attendances at Mass, particularly among men, young adults and the Australian-born; changing attitudes to forms of authority; and increasing reliance on personal experience as the foundation for belief and moral decision-making. This new '*modus vivendi*' has been recognised by Pope Francis who has said: "The defining characteristic of this change of epoch is that things are no longer in their place."[17]

---

17 See visnews-en.blogspot.com.au/2013/09/priests-to-face-epoch-change-as.html – accessed on 24 January 2014.

Part Three – Personal Reflections

This section includes the two most personal chapters as Michael McGirr and Andrew Hamilton SJ reflect on their own life journeys in the context of mission and identity, and a chapter in which Denis Fitzgerald reflects on the conference as a whole, and outlines the closing conference address by Bishop Eugene Hurley.

McGirr, in a paper based on his 2013 Mary MacKillop Oration, chooses the Australian saint Mary MacKillop as a model of a highly effective leader. He points us to her humour as a central element in her composure as a leader. Part of her enduring gift to us was her light-hearted spirit even in the heaviest of circumstances. She managed to avoid anxiety. Her vision of leadership was warm and expansive. Her gift was to get everyone "to eat at the same table" as Jesus did. Mary MacKillop, like Pope Francis, "calls us beyond our habits of fear. She urges us to set new limits". As Pope Francis says, going out into the streets in search of people will lead to accidental encounters, "but I prefer a thousand times over an accident-ridden Church to a sick Church".

Hamilton shows that our thoughts about mission and identity cannot be static. His own have evolved through various life experiences. He applauds the realism and enthusiasm with which those engaged in Catholic social services approach their task. Diversity is easily accepted and organisations are committed to being inclusive. Organisations exist for the people they serve. And he was encouraged by conference speakers who "acknowledge the reality of the world in which we work, the importance of good companions and the primacy of the mission to respect human dignity".

Appropriately, Hamilton finishes with Pope Francis whose vision is re-shaping the Catholic approach to mission and identity.

We must come together to transform the lives of people who are disadvantaged. To do this Catholics must live and work not at the comfortable centre of the Church but at its edges. Catholic identity must always be inclusive.

Fitzgerald reflects on some of the themes that were common across a number of speakers, such as the Gospel roots of our calling, and the invitation this extends to us; and the advantages and challenges of the diverse religious environment that is the reality for many Catholic social service providers. He argues that our mission and identity can only be robust as part of a sophisticated organisational dialogue, that draws on its Catholic features and roots, but encompasses all those engaged in bringing the mission to life. This is not easy, but is a challenge that must be faced, and the conference papers provide assistance to this endeavour.

Bishop Eugene Hurley's closing address to the conference was entitled "Challenged and Inspired to be Christ in the World Today". His call for faith-inspired engagement with the world neatly brought together key themes of other presenters. He drew heavily on his own experience of working with Indigenous communities, asylum seekers and others. And out of these encounters with the beloved of Christ, Bishop Eugene called on all to strive, with love, to close the chasm between the Church and Christ; to heal the wounds, warm the hearts, and be close to the people, since "the blazing glory of the Resurrection far surpasses any human weaknesses and their effects". It was a grand conference finale.

PART ONE

General Perspectives

1

The Heart of the Matter

Margaret Mary Flynn ibvm

Identity and Mission are the Heart of the Matter for all successful organisations and none more so than for faith-based organisations such as ours.

In focusing on these two key words, Identity and Mission, it is important from the start to ask whose identity and whose mission? The first point I want to make is that for faith-based organisations we do not have a mission, it is God's mission – and we collectively work in service of this one mission. The Church does not have a mission, CentaCare or CatholicCare does not have a mission, congregations do not have a mission. Our mission statements serve to articulate how each organisation seeks to serve God's mission within its particular context and through its specific ministries. The question then is how our sense of identity supports or hinders the service of God's mission. In this context, we need to reflect on both our personal identity, particularly as leaders, and also on the sense of identity within our organisations.

Jim Collins, noted expert and author on business and organisational matters suggests that there are three essential elements to a successful non-profit organisation, and these are:

- To know what we are deeply passionate about.
- To know what we are best in the world at.

- To know the resources needed.[18]

So, let us focus on the first essential – what are we deeply passionate about? What lies right at the Heart of the Matter? And where do we find a solid identity that underpins the wonderful mission we serve through our social services.

Take a minute and think what has brought you to your work in the field of social services or a similar ministry – right to the heart of the human condition – and what keeps you going?

I imagine it is a passion for justice, and a deep concern for those in need that form the basis of your personal commitment and also of your agency's mission statement. But if we are to drill down to the Heart of the Matter, then we need to go one step further to know, own and take responsibility for what inspires and sustains that commitment.

If it is first and foremost God's mission that we are to serve, then what does this require of us in terms of our identity? Surely it demands that we give regular time to savouring our experience of God, to reflecting on and sharing our spiritual inspiration, and supporting our staff to do the same.

We have a role model in Jesus, who was so sure he was responding fully to the mission of his God that he could confidently say "to have seen me, is to have seen the Father" (*John* 14: 9). I think this a key question we need to ask of ourselves and our organisations: Does seeing me … seeing us offer a glimpse of God to those with and for whom we work? This is what is being asked of us as people of the Gospel. Daunting, but true!

The passion Jesus brought to the service of God's mission was

---

18 Jim Collins, *Good to Great and the Social Sectors*, Random House, United Kingdom, 2006, p.19.

such that he did not hold back or allow the prevailing expectations and structures to prevent him from the personal encounters which brought healing to those in need. In fact he gave his life for it.

Now I am not suggesting that our roles need to kill us (though no doubt at times you think they will), but I do encourage you to think of yourselves as real followers of Jesus, and your staff as a community of disciples. They may not all be Catholic or Christian, but in my experience and particularly when in CentaCare Wilcannia-Forbes, where I was Director, most staff did believe in a God – a creator, lifegiver – and were energised when asked to relate their work to their belief. Whether they believed in Jesus or not, they were inspired by the values and principles by which he lived – really inspired because it tapped into their own desires and generosity.

As leaders, whether we like it or not, we are role models. For better or worse, our actions, our way of approaching life and issues will influence the workplace and its culture. It is therefore important that we ask ourselves what it is that we are modelling, and how often do we speak of our belief and the ways it fuels our passion for the work we do.

I loved our CentaCare Wilcannia-Forbes mission statement.[19] When we first developed it, I had not imagined the impact it would have on uniting us with great fervour for our very diverse ministries. These are some of the ways we used it:

- At induction, taking an hour or so with new staff for a conversation about the mission statement, what words or phrases struck them, and how this related to their own values. At the same time managers would share how our

---

19 See centacarewf.org.au/wp/wp-content/uploads/Our-CentaCare-story.pdf – accessed on 24 January 2014.

mission statement touched into their fundamental belief system and inspired the passion for their work.
- At least quarterly, at supervision, asking staff to reflect on how they saw their most recent work reflecting the mission statement.
- Managers using the mission statement as a tool to discern whether to apply for a new service. If the service did not adequately reflect the mission or its values, then we did not apply for it.

I believe that mission statement was fundamental in inspiring and sustaining the passion and our sense of corporate identity. It inspired staff to go the extra mile, to develop creative models of service that addressed the needs of their clients, to think and step outside the words on paper, to meet people in their context and at the point of their need. For an agency that was so far flung and with a myriad of small contracts for a variety of services, it was the one thing that gave us a sense of shared identity. It was the glue and the source of common inspiration and purpose.

The mission must be fired by passion! We need the salt to be salty. We know from a good source, what happens when it "becomes tasteless … it is good for nothing" (*Matthew* 5:13).

I wonder how we resonate with Dawna Markova when she declares:

> I will not die an unlived life.
> I will not live in fear
> of falling or catching fire.
> I choose to inhabit my days,
> to allow my living to open me,
> to make me less afraid,
> more accessible;

> to loosen my heart
> until it becomes a wing,
> a torch, a promise.
> I choose to risk my significance,
> to live so that which came to me as seed
> goes to the next as blossom,
> and that which came to me as blossom,
> goes on as fruit.[20]

I am sure many of you are aware of Margaret Wheatley, writer and management consultant who studies organisational behaviour. In her book, *Perseverance*, she writes of the importance of knowing the ground we stand on – knowing what we believe and the foundations of our sense of identity.

She writes:

> Do you know the ground you stand on? How well do you know its strengths, its pitfalls, the places that give you courage, the places where you get stuck? Do you know where to find your ground when things get bad? Do you pay it any attention when things are good?
>
> Nobody gets through life ungrounded. Unless we know this and are conscious of the ground we stand on, we may be shocked to discover that what appeared as granite is, in fact, quicksand.[21]

To know our ground – not just to know it, but to experience it in the depths of our being – being so sure of our mission and the beliefs that inspire it, is crucial:

- it provides an anchor when life gets tough (and believe

---

20 Dawna Markova, *Reclaiming Purpose and Passion*, Conari Press, California, 2000.
21 Margaret J. Wheatley, *Perseverance*, Berrett-Koehler Publishers, San Francisco, 2010, p. 37.

me, I know how tough it can get on so many levels – with contractual obligations, industrial issues, financial viability, competition, uncertainty of renewal of contracts),
- it fires the passion that inspires exceptional generosity and care, and
- it gives flight to creativity and a belief in possibility.

So how do we nurture and sustain this inspiration? How do we ensure that our deep sense of identity is nurtured in lives that are so busy, constantly confronted by new and varied experiences, good and bad? The answer to this, I believe, lies in the very title of this conference: "Listening, Learning and Leading".

As we grow and change, one would trust that our experience of God and our sense of identity would also change over time, and if it is this which inspires our passion for the mission, then we need to keep visiting what truly lies in our hearts. We need to be constantly listening, learning from the new insights both spiritual and ministry-focussed, and leading by the way we relate and through inspirational conversation.

It is helpful to notice how regularly Jesus withdrew from the demands of his ministry to be in touch with his God, to deepen that relationship and to seek inspiration from it.

As Margaret Wheatley advises:

> Ground has to be cultivated. We create ground by nurturing our convictions, by learning from our experience ... We have to take time to learn and reflect, stepping out of the fray to observe it periodically.[22]

Knowing our ground, and knowing it well, consciously

---

22 Ibid.

attending to it and taking good care – this is the only way to withstand turbulence.

Even the most outrageous stream has a muddy bed that serves to keep it within bounds, enabling it to find its way to the sea.[23]

How we do this as individuals and as work teams is up to us, but it is at our peril not to do so. The greater the demands of the workplace and the complexity of all that surrounds us, the greater the need to take time out, to reflect on our experience, and to tap into what is the ground of our being. We know as leaders, it is who we are, it is the vibes we give out and what we represent that are as significant as our organisational or management endeavours.

The clear message here is that to sustain a strong mission-focussed identity, we as leaders need to make time to be in touch with our fundamental inspiration, to create opportunities for our staff communities to do the same, and to encourage conversations at this level.

It seems there is nothing static in all of this. Just as in the service of God's mission, we need to keep tending to our sense of identity, so this identity will impact on the way we serve the mission – how we develop models of service that best respond to the dignity of those we serve, and which most respectfully and effectively bring healing and hope.

The question remains, how do we balance the fire for God's mission with the inexorable demands of compliance, staffing issues, contractual and political uncertainties and all the practical matters that present and need constant attention?

Tony Gittins, theologian and anthropologist, speaks of an

---

23 Ibid., p. 46.

essential tension that is needed within the context of the service of God's mission – a tension between two polar opposites which he identifies as communitas and community. He defines 'communitas', as that passionate commitment to living the Gospel, "marked by zeal and energy, enthusiasm and collaboration", and contrasts this with 'community', the institutionalisation of communitas which he suggests "is as necessary as it is inevitable being structured, conservative and routine". [24]

As Gittins says:

> Communitas produces the energy for takeoff; community sustains level flight. Communitas produces dreams and visions; community maintains works and programs that keep dreams alive and creates strategies that service the vision.
>
> Both communitas and community are necessary for long-term undertakings. But in the long term, renewal can only come from a rediscovery of communitas since community lacks the imagination and fire required by true conversion.
>
> When the flame dies, when the spark fails, when the fuel is depleted, no coal will produce heat, no flint flame and no rocket liftoff.[25]

This is hardly revolutionary, but I believe it does hold a significant challenge for us leading and working in faith-based agencies. How do we hold these two dynamics in tension? How do we prevent the expectations of funding bodies, the competitive landscape and traditional expectations from stifling a Gospel response to those in need?

In the latest Catholic Social Services Australia annual report, Fr Joe

---

24 Anthony Gittins, *A Presence that Disturbs,* Liguori/Triumph, Liguori, Mo., 2002, p. 78.
25 Ibid.

Caddy quotes Pope Francis who made this pithy comment in a recent address: "We cannot become starched Christians, too polite, who speak of theology calmly over tea. We have to become courageous Christians and seek out those who need help most."[26] I would add, not just to seek out those who need help most, but to place them at the centre of our models of service and the service network.

As I reflect back on my time with CentaCare I wonder when and how we allowed bureaucratic and contractual expectations to hold us back from being fully present to the needs of individuals, and accompanying them through the morass of the service network. It is interesting that we received the greatest interest and support from Government funding bodies for models of practice that were not just innovative, but which engaged people in their own context, and learned from them what would be most helpful.

A number of departmental people have said to me over the years: "Margaret, we don't know where to go next, we're uninspired, we need the service providers to give us the models."

The most fundamental question for us is who or what drives our service provision – who or what is at the centre? Is it finance, desperation to fulfil contractual numbers, or is it the client – the human person. If we agree that it is the client, then we must also agree that it is about relationship. Relationship by definition requires a mutual listening and learning, and from the service provider perspective, a humility and respectful recognition of all the client brings to the encounter.

Pope Benedict XVI in his encyclical *Deus Caritas Est* stressed the need for a "formation of the heart"[27] for those who work in this field, for as he states:

---

26 Joe Caddy, *Catholic Social Services Australia Annual Report 2012-2013*, p. 4.
27 Pope Benedict XVI, Encyclical Letter, *Deus Caritas Est*, St Pauls Publications, Strathfield, 2006, p. 53.

> While professional competence is a primary, fundamental requirement, it is not of itself sufficient. We are dealing with human beings, and human beings always need something more than technically proper care. They need humanity. They need heartfelt concern ... enabling them to experience the richness of their humanity.[28]

This sentiment is echoed by Claude Marie Barbour when he writes:

> When ministry is seen as dialogical, it means that ministers become persons immersed in the world of others, like Jesus was in our world. It is with people, therefore, that the minister begins to ask questions; it is with people that basic human values are endorsed and challenged; and it is this context that shapes the way of announcing the good news and of denouncing sinful structures.[29]

Sadly, many of the structures we have within our own agencies and certainly within the whole welfare space present a silo approach which can so easily further disempower the client. For the marginalised who already experience disadvantage and powerlessness vis-à-vis more dominant sections of the community, we need to be so careful that an experience of the social services sector does not further compound their multiple deprivation. The silo model is mainly driven by the requirements of government contracts, but we need to ask to what extent are we prepared to give the government more authority than the Gospel? Is it possible that Catholic Social Services would dare to risk new and more compassionate and relational models which place the client at the centre of our concern and that of the service network?

---

28 Ibid., p. 52.
29 Stephen B. Bevans and Roger P. Schroeder, *Prophetic Dialogue: Reflections on Christian Mission Today*, Orbis Books, New York, 2011, p. 75.

I want to leave you with this question while we move to a much larger context for our sense of mission and identity. For this I am asking you to come with me on a brief journey into the universe. I do this, because our understanding of how the universe works very much impacts on how we understand ourselves, how we relate to others and how we understand God.

Way back in the 13th century, St Thomas Aquinas stated: "A mistake in our understanding of creation will necessarily cause a mistake in our understanding of God."[30]

Right now, we are at a stage in human history where our traditional understandings of God are being called into question. The new sciences and the new spiritualities are forcing us, however unwillingly, to look afresh at who God is for us, and therefore have implications for our sense of identity and our approach to ministry.

From the 17th century and until quite recently, we in the West have been very much influenced by the classical Newtonian cosmology or worldview – a cosmological mindset shaped by the classical science and physics of that era.

Looking at reality through a Newtonian lens, the world was seen as static and mechanistic. It presented the world as a collection of inert objects that obeyed predictable laws and, in doing so, effectively presented a closed system that removed relational Mystery from the workings of the everyday. It gave us the prevailing theory of the universe as an ordered whole and the general laws that govern it.

And it is not too hard to see how this worldview has influenced the Western psyche including the way we structure our service provision.

Creation too was understood as well-ordered and mechanistic,

---

30 St Thomas Aquinas, *Summa Contra Gentiles* II. 2. 3.

each element with its place and a hierarchy of being – heaven … earth … and the underworld.

This mechanistic world view and theology served to create dichotomies which continue to influence so much of our understanding of life – and contribute to unhelpful divisions and the silos we tend to create and accept.

Now at the beginning of the 21st century we are, according to many, in a period of cosmological transition. We appear to be moving out of the prevailing Newtonian mindset into one being shaped by the discoveries coming out of what is being termed the 'new science' – new discoveries in biology, chaos or complexity theory, astro- and quantum physics – which are changing our understanding of the way the world around us works and how we function within it.

The scientific community is now describing the physical cosmos not as a static, inert machine but as a mysterious relational entity which is still becoming, whose promise, we might say, is yet to be fulfilled. Findings in the field of quantum mechanics, for example, are creating a very different chapter in our perception of the cosmos and the laws that govern it, one which challenges and moves beyond the cold, mechanistic Newtonian conceptions. Subatomic particles, current science tells us, only come into form and are observed as they are in relationship to something else. They do not exist as independent 'things'. So in the quantum world discrete 'things' are replaced by 'patterns of active relationship', systems and processes that create dense webs of connection.

These findings are presenting us with a world that requires new metaphors. Some scientists speak about a continuous dance of energy where everything is connected, and the universe being more like a great thought than a great machine. What seems clear is that we have reached a point in time where new understandings and insights from science are connecting us more deeply to the greater web of life of which we are a part.

Judy Cannato, a woman among many others making the links between the new scientific understandings and theology, suggests:

> On an unconscious yet collective level, we are connected to all that is happening on the planet. We are constantly influencing and being influenced, entraining and resonating, emitting positive or negative energy, affecting and being affected by all that is. Although we may think we function as separate persons, at every second we are caught in a web of interconnected and interdependent relationships that shape what we call reality.[31]

I suggest that we take the bold step to enter this exploration, to listen to what it might say to us about the Divine, about the responsibility we have to influence the energies around us, and the way we develop our models of service. If it is true that we are all caught up in this dynamic dance of energy, then it seems as leaders we are not only role models, but have the added responsibility of ensuring that the energies we are constantly putting out, whether we know it or not, are positive and inspirational. Again, this demands ongoing self-reflection and responsibility for our identity.

To quote Judy Cannato once again:

> We tend to believe that most of us cannot and do not make much difference in the great scheme of things. The reality is that, noticed or not, every conscious act that gives witness to the new possibilities and greater awareness contributes to the transformation of the whole …
>
> No matter what we do, we are always affecting the energy around us, in either a negative or positive way.

---

31 Judy Cannato, *Field of Compassion*, Sorin Books, Indiana, 2010, p. 140.

> Why should we not then become aware of our power and choose consciously rather than unconsciously how we will shape our world?[32]

Regarding the impact on what we do and how we do it, does there not seem to be a clear parallel between the mechanistic world view, and some of the approaches found both within our own agencies and the social services network as a whole? To continue with isolated, siloed approaches within a world made of dynamic flows of relational energy can only lead to debilitating discord, a constant sapping of our energies, and limited service effectiveness. Of all areas of work, surely it is those focussed on the wellbeing of the person, that we must keep pushing to find the most respectfully relational and empowering models of support.

Within the social services area, it is both the individual service provider and the whole system that needs to be called into a more dynamic dance which provides holistic support to the client and sets them at the centre. I believe there is great potential here for our agencies to take the initiative to work with government and the wider social services network in developing models of service which are more respectful of the lives and context of the marginalised.

This reminds me of examples we met in Wilcannia-Forbes. We would hear organisations bemoaning the fact that their statistics were down and being very critical of potential clients who were not making appointments for themselves or their children. We were also aware of situations where clients were lost and overwhelmed within the forest of siloed services – being told to make appointments with several disconnected agencies where they would need to tell their story over and over again.

---

32 Ibid., p. 6.

Surely there is a more relational way of being and of serving which ensures that the client is partnered within a dynamic and connected service network throughout their dance of healing. This can be done in the simplest of ways, but first we must be prepared to step out of our own silos and enter the context of the client.

Let me give a couple of very simple examples from life out west. In our work with Aboriginal mothers, we would constantly hear the complaint of Community Health services that children were not being brought to the clinic for immunisation. Our Aboriginal Family Worker who held playgroup in a park near where many families lived, invited the health nurse to come to the park, and within half a day most children had received the necessary vaccinations.

During the last drought we, like many rural agencies, received funding for drought support. Rather than waiting for farming families to make appointments for counselling or to attend a talk on depression, the drought worker went out to badly affected areas, got farmers to organise barbecues at farmgate gatherings, and at another time organised a series of creative welding workshops in different farming neighbourhoods. At both types of gatherings, in their natural setting, the farmers engaged in conversations about life, had input from a series of service providers on issues related to health and mental health, and had health checks. Through this process they became more sensitive to their own needs as well as the wellbeing of their neighbours, and a number continued to connect with the service providers they had met.

These examples are two among many that show the importance and impact of ministry that enters the experience of the client, places the service provider within the client context and supports non-threatening human encounter and relational mutuality. I know many Catholic Social Services and other such organisations would have similar stories to tell, but the Gospel call us to go further, to take risks which ensure the human person, and particularly the vulnerable, are shepherded with respect and love – within our agencies, the service network and the wider community.

We live in exciting times, so let us keep them spiced and well-salted with a passion that allows us to dare to risk new ways in the service of God's mission – new ways of relating to those who are most vulnerable. This is indeed the Heart of the Matter – that those who see us ... may increasingly see God.

2

Called to Lead: Leadership to Make Mission a Reality

Chris Lowney

Compare today to 1985: the world has become faster paced and more complicated; it is characterised by more change and more decisions. That is why we need to focus on leadership.[33]

When I started at JP Morgan in 1983 and we used the word 'leadership', a person came to mind: the chief executive of JP Morgan. But then during the 1990s and 2000s, the world started to become faster paced and more complex, and we appreciated that we had to think about leadership less in terms of one person or a small group of people, and more as a 'behaviour' that was needed throughout the organisation: the chief executive alone could no longer make every important decision, represent the company's values to all constituents, make the tough ethical calls, and so on.

Rather, we understood that we needed a widespread culture of leadership, and so it is with all your Catholic social services organisations, for the very same reasons of change, complexity, the multiplicity of decisions, and so on. That culture of leadership is not a choice or a fad; it is simply a fact of organisational life in the current maelstrom of a world.

But what does good leadership actually look like? What qualities,

---

33 For a more detailed exploration of leadership, see Chris Lowney, *Heroic Leadership: Best Practices from a 450-Year-Old Company That Changed the World*, Loyola Press, Chicago, 2005.

behaviours or attributes do you associate with leading well? A leader can conceive of and convey some real sense of the future – where we need to go and is able to motivate, inspire and align us around this vision of the future. By doing so, and by dealing with unforeseen obstacles that come up along the way, the great leader drives needed and desired change in the organisation and the world.

Who Are Leaders?

So who are leaders? I guess, if most of us answered a question like this, we would think of the Prime Minister, the Pope and so on. I wonder how many of you would put forward your own name. I suspect virtually no-one. Why not? The answer might have something to do with modesty, a laudable virtue. We associate leadership with being in charge, famous, a celebrity, and are too modest to associate ourselves with that stereotype. But, though the modesty is essential, the stereotype is broken. And in some ways, the first persons we each should consider leaders are ourselves. And I will explain how.

And what do effective leaders do to motivate those around them? Here is an idea ventured by a man who himself compiled unimpeachable credentials as a leader. His simple, succinct vision: "You must love those you lead before you can be an effective leader." The leader just quoted is General Eric K. Shinseki, recently retired US Army Chief of Staff.

Sentiment like his may seem a bit remarkable and even out of place among the military class. But I suspect that a general makes wiser choices when he loves those he must place in harm's way, and I suspect that soldiers perform more effectively when confident that they are loved and valued by those tasked with the awful burden of sending them to face possible death. Note that even the military, which we most typically associate with an hierarchical style of leadership, perhaps especially the military, understands that our most important claim to leadership is not our status or hierarchical position on an organisational chart, but the values we choose to role model – like love in the case of General Shinseki, quoted above.

This concept of leadership – that it has to do with the values that all of us exhibit – certainly may run counter to our cultural stereotypes, but it is neither gimmickry nor something I have made up. In considering the above-mentioned qualities associated with leadership, hierarchical leaders tend to spring to mind, but the qualities, for the most part, have nothing to do with hierarchy. They are values that anyone in your organisation could role model, from the most junior position to the most senior, from someone who manages no-one to the chief executive.

In fact, one of your tasks as leaders of Catholic social services, in a fast changing, complex world, is to spread a broad culture of leadership throughout your organisations. And when you tell your subordinates they need to show leadership, most will be confused. They will think: "Wait a minute: she hires the people, I don't. She manages the budget and makes the strategy, I don't. What is she on about?" Doing an exercise with your staff on shared values and 'shared' leadership may lead to a 'light bulb' moment: "Aha! I show leadership around here by role modelling the leadership values we all care about." In fact, one of the dictionary definitions of leadership reinforces this same broad concept of leadership, which is defined as "the act of pointing out a way, direction, or goal and influencing others toward it".

Everyone working in Catholic social services – for better or worse – is doing this all the time. You are pointing out a way or a direction for your colleagues, friends and neighbours by how you treat those you work with or for and those you meet, how you prioritise your time, and so on – in other words, you are leading. Many of you are parents: can there be any more obvious act of pointing out a way and influencing others than the leadership that you are showing with your children every day?

Though all of us are leading, many of us are doing so only 'subconsciously'. And I want to invite each of you to become more purposeful, to think about yourselves as having a leadership opportunity and responsibility, and then to think what values you will exemplify as the leadership statement that will be your life.

Leadership as Profoundly Spiritual

Now, a lot of us tend to think of leadership as a secular concept. It is like the 'business stuff' that former bankers like Lowney ramble on about, and it feels a bit alien to our works, which are deeply mission-driven, and often deeply religious. But I want to make the case that the idea of leadership is, in fact, profoundly spiritual, and we can find a call to a particular kind of leadership deeply rooted in the Judaeo-Christian tradition, and let me take that on upfront. I guess that most people would describe themselves in religious terms first of all as *followers*: we are followers of Jesus. And indeed, our religious language uses words like vocation and disciple that have a sense of following. But our religious language also uses words like apostle and mission, and those words have a very different sense, the idea of sending or being sent.

The sixth chapter of *Isaiah* offers a wonderful meditation on what we might call the mystery of leadership in a religious context. You will recall that the chapter begins with the prophet's confession of his own perceived unworthiness and fault: "Woe is me. For I am lost, for I am a man of unclean lips…" He is, however, touched in some way by the Divine Presence and, when he hears the voice of the Lord, "Whom shall I send? Who will go for us?", he is able to answer: "Here I am, send me." Much of that chapter reflects what I might call the mystery of leadership within the context of religious vocation. We all tend to associate leadership with prominence, power, certainty, clarity, decisiveness, yet the one called to lead in *Isaiah* seems anything but certain at first.

I was recently at a conference for board chairs and chief executive officers of US healthcare systems, and one presenter said that, precisely because of the complexity and change with which we are living, we are all moving from an era of 'paradigm' to one of 'paradox', and that boards have to be willing to live with "shared uncertainty". This is in many ways a new 'skill' for all of us: to accept the intimidating levels of unknown we have to live with, yet – and this is important – still be willing to accept our accountability for making decisions and moving forward.

Our own path to successful leadership must follow the same pattern as Isaiah's: first, knowing ourselves well, including our weaknesses and faults. Then, feeling ourselves in some ways called, sustained, touched, which is what enables us to feel willing to say every morning: "Here I am, send me." Unless we have this kind of a spirituality of leadership, I would suggest, leadership becomes all about us; we can become cynical and bitter because things do not go the way we want. Instead, if we are sustained, we become capable of leadership for the long term. In fact, great leadership is fundamentally spiritual, and I say this to chief executives all the time, regardless of whether they have religious beliefs or not. And when they are sceptical I use their own business language to prove it to them.

If any of you are accounting-literate, you know that your headquarters' building and other facilities have a value on your organisation's accounts. The building is tangible, and we can measure its value and count up the dollar value of the organisation's assets. But you also know that your employees have essentially no value in accounting, other than perhaps some accrued pension. However, every chief executive, even in the most materialistic industry on earth, knows that, in fact, just the opposite is true: the building is really value-less unless the people who walk into it every day have some powerful sense of purpose, work hard, are committed, will help each other, treat each other with respect, and a dozen other things that separate great organisations from terrible ones.

And let me mention two of these traits of what we might call 'spirituality of leadership' – firstly, a sense of purpose greater than self (I sometimes call it heroism) and secondly, deep self-awareness and a habit of reflection. I will then conclude with some reflections on Pope Francis and his invitation to all of us to get our feet dusty.

A Spirit of Heroism – A Sense of Purpose Greater than Self

We have grown accustomed to associating the idea of heroism with extraordinary acts like saving persons trapped in burning buildings or saving comrades in battle. But most of us cannot control the opportunities that life will present to us: we may never have the chance to save someone in distress. The only thing we always control, on the other hand, is our *response* to whatever opportunities life gives us. And let us be frank, for most of us, the opportunities life gives are small. The teacher or social worker has no guarantee that he or she will make a profound, life-altering impact in a child's life: his or her heroism is manifest in the commitment to live and work as if he or she *might* make such a difference.

In fact, many of us must suffer moments of doubt that our work makes any meaningful, visible impact in another person's life.

One moral theologian defines mercy as "the willingness to enter the chaos of another person's life". And so it is for many of us. We are mercifully entering chaotic family situations where financial stresses, dysfunctional systems, substance abuse issues, and a host of other challenges all conspire to frustrate tangible progress in making a difference. Our heroism in such circumstances is our continued commitment and enthusiasm to try.

Another quality of this kind of heroism is the appreciation that one is part of some larger mission. Let me illustrate this with an anecdote from the US space program of the 1960s, when Russia and the US were racing to get a rocket to the moon. There is an anecdote that President Kennedy visited NASA, met a gentleman sweeping the floors and, to be polite, asked him what his job was. He supposedly replied: "Sir, I'm putting a man on the moon." Let me tell you another 'man on the moon' story, directly like it: a janitor at one of the Catholic hospitals in the US happened to enter a room where a woman was sitting with her mother, who was dying. And I guess it was a somewhat emotional moment, and the woman asked the janitor if he would say a little prayer for the dying mother. So here is what the janitor says: "Oh, I always pray for each patient family as I clean each day."

I am from New York City, and we are a little too jaundiced for such sweet stories. But even I know that the teams which perform best are teams where people 'get over themselves', and appreciate that they are part of some worthy mission that is greater than themselves. It is not all about being the marketing person, the chief finance officer, the teacher, the janitor: rather, organisations succeed only when each of these folks sees him- or herself as contributing to some greater purpose. That is, of course, a deeply spiritual idea, very familiar in the Christian tradition, where we are raised with the vision that we are here to serve God's plan for humanity, to serve our neighbour, not ourselves.

But this is also a business idea. I am sure some of you are familiar with *Good to Great*, in which Jim Collins and his researchers tried to point to some characteristics that separated mediocre companies from outstanding ones.[34] The first quality he points to is that great companies have what he calls 'level 5' leaders, people who are willing to put the cause, the mission, ahead of their own ego. That is very much what the above means and it is fascinating that he confesses that he really does not know how that quality develops in people. Well, I think we in the faith-based world often do know how this purpose greater than self-spirit develops in people. Often it is the fruit of self-awareness, my next area of focus.

Self-awareness and Leadership

Anyone who has managed lots of people or worked in human resources – I have done both – has been mystified by the phenomenon of rising stars who later 'crash and burn', even though they had the total package of technical skills, smarts, ambition and training. One school of thought attributes these spectacular flame-outs to lack of self-awareness: those with talent who bomb out frequently have it too easy in the beginning, and never come to grips with their values and weaknesses. They do very well when all we ask them to do is move numbers around spreadsheets. But they start to fail as soon as we ask them to do grown-up things, like dealing with human beings or with problems that do not have easy solutions. And we have all learned in life that most problems do not have easy solutions. And so we need people with judgment – the ability to look at various sub-

---

[34] Jim Collins, *Good to Great: Why Some Companies Make the Leap ... and Others Don't*, HarperBusiness, New York, 2001.

optimal alternative paths of action and to reason why one might be better than the others. And then, with courage, to go forward with that course of action even though they do not have mathematical certainty they are correct, to assume some risk of failure, the risk of looking foolish in front of peers if they are wrong.

And you may know that one school of thought attributes this inability to develop judgment and courage to a lack of self-awareness. What sometimes happens is that very smart people easily learn how to 'do school', but they never learn how to 'do life'. Things come too easily in the beginning, and they never learn the resiliency that comes with having to fail and keep going, how to accept feedback from others, and so on. The Harvard emeritus Abraham Zaleznik once observed that many leaders seem to be individuals who were 'twice born', where some personal crisis like injury, alcoholism or bankruptcy forced them to come to grips as adults with who they were and what they valued and wanted. And his thesis was that it was precisely their crises that accounted for their long-term success.

And I guess I want to extract a few related points about self-awareness: one, if life does not thrust a crisis on us, we all need to create mechanisms to come to grips in some deep way with who we are, what we stand for, and so on. This is an area where we, as faith-based organisations, should have a real 'competitive advantage' relative to secular businesses. JP Morgan does not have any particular tradition of how to grow deep self-awareness in individuals, but every religious tradition does: through prayer, self-reflection, retreat-type experiences and so on. In order to get more effective in the 'business' of our ministry, so to speak, we need to take more advantage of some of the spiritual tools that are part of our traditions.

The second learning I would extract about self-awareness is this: many of those we serve in our welfare agencies have to confront great challenge and difficulty in their lives: poverty, poor family structures, inadequate education, etc. And I suspect many of our workers, especially junior ones, also face great challenge: for example, the disillusionment of not being able to make a difference sometimes, or of failing, or of feeling helpless. We tend to see only the negative dimension of such experiences but, in light of the above, we might also see these as fertile ground to help our own employees and those we serve to grow in the kind of self-awareness that leads to more effective self-leadership. In that way, such challenge can also be seen in its redemptive aspects, as a source of developing resiliency and depth.

So, to lead well, we all need to make some profound investment in knowing ourselves, and then we also need some kind of mechanism to keep ourselves updated every day on how we are doing. And here, once again, our faith-based tradition can be a source of 'competitive advantage' so to speak, in our efforts to be effective in work.

As a Jesuit in the seminary, I learned a wonderfully modern and easy-to-adopt tool for daily updating. Each Jesuit follows a daily regimen of one or two mental 'pit stops' that in aggregate might absorb as little as fifteen minutes a day. Take a quiet five minutes, for example, once after lunch and once before going to bed, and do three things. First, remind yourself of what you have to be grateful for. Second, raise your horizon a bit. Remind yourself of your goals – which might be a weakness you want to work on or an objective to achieve, or your sense of mission as a person. And third, mentally scroll through the last few hours to extract lessons learned from your performance that might help in the next few hours: if you were irritated all morning, what was happening? Can you focus on that, get over it, and then get back to living in the present.

I think the genius of this simple practice is obvious when we consider its origins. Jesuits broke radically from existing custom when they started: by abandoning the monastic practice of gathering together in chapel multiple times daily to pray the liturgy of the hours in common, in order instead to pursue a much more activist lifestyle. Yet, the founder of the Jesuits, St Ignatius of Loyola, had the incredibly modern insight that we in the 21st century typically overlook: if you and I do not have the luxury of retreating to chapel multiple times daily like monks, we need to find some other way of keeping ourselves focused and recollected as we bob along each day on a tide of e-mails, phone calls, and meetings without ever pulling back to take stock. I am sure you have seen the fallout from this chaotic lifestyle as I have: the person who gets to the end of the day without ever getting to his or her 'number 1' priority, or the person who has a meeting go badly at 8.30am and remains distracted about it all day, draining productivity. These are self-awareness problems, and our spiritual traditions give us a great tool for coping. It is a religious practice, of course, but we see how our religious disciplines can also have very powerful worldly payoffs.

In conclusion, I want to plant one other key theme, drawing on the life history of our new Pope to do so.

The Leadership of Pope Francis

I have recently published a book about Pope Francis, *Pope Francis: Why He Leads the Way He Leads*.[35] In its preparation I was lucky enough to be able to talk to a number of Jesuits who lived with him when he was 'just' Fr Bergoglio, who told me stories about the Pope 'before the cameras were rolling', so to speak. And I took away a lot of great

---

35 Chris Lowney, *Pope Francis: Why He Leads the Way He Leads*, Loyola Press, Chicago, 2013.

images. One of these Jesuits retains an image of Bergoglio at 5.30 in the morning pitching laundry into a big industrial washing machine, doing his share of the chores even though he was the rector – the boss – and his subordinates were a few dozen seminarians.

Another one of them told me a story that helps tie together some of what I have discussed. He said that Bergoglio, while he was rector of the seminary, was asked to assume responsibility for a new parish in an impoverished community and drafted some seminarian volunteers to assist him. To do what? Well, walk the neighbourhood. Bergoglio told them, using an Argentine expression that might very loosely be paraphrased in English as follows: "Don't skim the cream". In other words, do not focus only on the people who like you or who go to Church or with whom it is easy to work: meet everyone. "Seek out the poorest and see what could be done to help them," he said, and he also told them: "Just remember, you are going to learn from the poor before you teach them anything." When the seminarians returned from these visits, Fr Bergoglio used to check whose shoes were dusty: who was showing the frontier spirit to meet people where they really live.

After the team discovered just how poor their neighbours were, one Jesuit remembers Bergoglio saying something like: "We can't just sit around here with our arms crossed while we have everything and those people don't even have enough food to eat." So, they took action, putting a big pot in a field to launch a primitive soup kitchen. This restlessly energetic, outgoing, innovative style is fundamental to the 'frontier spirit' Pope Francis wants to instil in our Church, and those in Catholic social services are on the frontiers. You are doing exactly what we should be doing.

Remember I just spoke about taking those two mental 'pit stops', the examen, the habit of prayerful reflection each day. Well, that discipline is valuable and essential when we are really immersed in the world, dealing with the sufferings, joys and problems of our neighbours. In his homily on the day after his election, Pope Francis said: "Our life is a journey, and when we stop moving, things go wrong." Well, if you are still all day and removed from the world, you do not need a contemplative break: you need the contemplative break precisely because you are so engaged.

In other words, such leaders are living a kind of paradoxical dynamic: fully immersed in the world, they are in touch; they are not afraid of plunging into problems; they are not sterile people living only in a world of ideology and theory. But at the very same time, they are not of the world. They step back, nourish themselves in prayer and reflection, take in the big perspective, remember to be grateful.

Some of you have surely read the remarkable interviews that Pope Francis gave in August 2013. And I was really struck by one thing, namely when he said he wants a Church that is "the home of all, not a small chapel that can hold only a small group of selected people".[36]

And when he visits refugees on Lampedusa, embraces the disabled in Vatican Square, says he wants a Church that is "for the poor", or encourages us to spread word of God's mercy, I think he is implicitly saying that our chapel is still too small. We have not yet made it a home for all, and fixing that is everyone's job. And those who are working in Catholic social services are really on the front lines of doing exactly that, helping to make our home bigger by working on the frontiers.

And by doing so, you are showing great leadership. And that is not just my opinion; it is also that of Pope Francis. Because also in that

---

36 Pope Francis, interview by Antonio Spadaro SJ on 19 August 2103; accessed on 27 January 2014 at vatican.va.

interview, he said that bishops "must be able to accompany the flock that has a flair for finding new paths". So let us get our shoes dusty; let us start finding new paths; let us live heroically; and let us embrace our leadership vocation.

3

Sharing the Mission with the Whole Organisation

Julie Edwards

Those involved in Catholic social services we will be familiar with the Gospel passage in *Matthew* (25: 35-37, 40) where Jesus says: "I was hungry and you gave me something to eat, I was thirsty and you gave me something to drink, I was a stranger and you invited me in, I needed clothes and you clothed me, I was sick and you looked after me, I was in prison and you visited me ... truly, whatever you did for the least of your brothers and sisters, you did for me." That is extremely challenging – to feed the hungry, to welcome the stranger, to visit the prisoner and so on.

We hear this challenge as individuals and we take it on board as individuals – that is difficult enough, but what about an organisation taking up the challenge? What would that look like? How do you go about getting an organisation, in all facets of its activities, to respond to the challenge and to operate and practise in this spirit?

If an organisation and its people are truly to do that and not simply an activity (good as that may be), then entering into relationship with the other in the spirit of Matthew's Gospel is critical. There has to be an alignment between who we are (our human spirit), what we do and how we go about our work (our practice), and how we operate as an organisation (business processes).

Living the Gospel, living authentically – justly, compassionately, lovingly – is always going to be a personal thing. It comes down to me, to you. There is no escaping that. But we are also communal; we are relationship people. We organise ourselves into groups, organisations and institutions. In keeping with the Catholic Social Teaching principle of subsidiarity whereby decisions and activities are undertaken at the most appropriate, effective level, it is often when we mobilise people, when there is a group, an organisation, that we can be most effective in delivering the desired outcome. So how do we go about achieving this?

Informed by my experiences 'on the ground' this chapter presents insights into how Jesuit Social Services has gone about making the mission something that is owned by the whole organisation. As the chapter has a focus on faith-based organisations, about the value of such agencies understanding their roots and continuing to bring them to life in a contemporary way, I want to make some qualifying statements at the outset.

Nothing 'magic' happens in terms of living out our mission just because we say we are a faith-based organisation or because we put a crucifix up on the wall, paint a logo on our door, or display inspirational values in our entrance foyer. These may reflect a particular way of doing things in our organisation but, in and of themselves, they do not guarantee anything. I have had the experience of working with strong social justice activists and people who profess deep faith but who treated colleagues and others terribly. I work with people who profess no religious faith but who are the most wonderful examples of our values in action, through their behaviour.

The mission will be evident in things like how we treat each other, our commitment to those most in need, how we conduct our meetings, how we manage our resources. The scandal of sexual abuse in the Church and its institutions (and the subsequent mishandling of this) should leave us in no doubt that there can be a big distance between what we profess and reality. It is important that we do not assume we have a monopoly on goodness or that professing a particular mission automatically produces a mission-based organisation. But we do have treasures in our spirituality and our founding stories, in Catholic Social Teaching, in our missions, and we can draw on these to inspire, shape and sustain us.

Jesuit Social Services

Before I explore what we can do to ensure that the mission is alive, real and owned by the whole organisation, let me tell you a little about Jesuit Social Services[37] where we seek to respond to the challenge in Matthew's Gospel and have been refining our ideas and approach to this for a number of years.

Jesuit Social Services is a social change organisation with a vision of building a just society. We believe that working collaboratively with others is key to achieving this vision and we therefore seek to influence hearts and minds to that end.

- Our mission is to stand in solidarity with those in need, and to express a faith that promotes justice.
- Our values are welcoming, discerning and courageous.
- Our purpose is that all people get the opportunity to live to their full potential.

We go where hope is most needed. We provide practical programs supporting people to learn, train and take up employment opportunities so they can realise their potential and be active, contributing and valued members of the community. We work at the hard end of social

---

37 See www.jss.org.au.

justice, with the following areas of focus:

- justice and crime prevention, e.g., working with people released from prison;
- settlement and community building for new arrivals, refugees and asylum seekers;
- mental health and wellbeing, providing services to people with mental illness and a range of other problems like drug dependence and homelessness and who have often experienced neglect, abuse and trauma from an early age.

Across all this work we aim to put people on a learning and employment pathway in order to help them participate more fully in the community.

Jesuit Social Services has some 200 staff and 200 volunteers. They are more or less representative of the broader community in terms of characteristics like faith and cultural background.

So, how do we go about having an organisation (not just a 'bunch' of people, good people, doing good things, but an organisation) whose very purpose informs all aspects of who we are, what we do and how we do it? How do we have a community organisation that is truly an Ignatian organisation in the Catholic tradition? And how do we do that in a way that is respectful of from where each one comes, that is invitational and not impositional? How do we build a culture in the organisation so that it is everyone's business?

There are a few things about which we need to be very clear and they start with our identity. Who are we? And this brings us to our purpose, why do we exist? What is our vision? Our mission?

And it is one thing to have that clear – on paper, up on the wall, in our collateral and our annual report – and it is another to have the mission as a 'living, breathing thing'. And that 'living, breathing thing' is our culture. So, how do you go about building a culture that sees everybody in the organisation having a sense of responsibility for the mission? I like to think of the organisation in ecological terms, as a living organism.

At Jesuit Social Services we have a number of ways of thinking and speaking about this. But one, which you might find helpful, is the image of a tree. The tree is an important symbol across cultures and spiritual traditions. It speaks to the interconnectedness of all

Figure 1: Jesuit Social Services' Tree Sculpture

life, the seen and unseen. The tree sculpture in Figure 1 symbolises Jesuit Social Services' strong foundations in its deep roots, drawing nourishment and inspiration from its Ignatian spirituality and heritage and the founding story, which animate our vision, our mission and our values.

The trunk of the tree represents our identity, culture and people – this is the solid, visible heart of the organisation. The branches reflect how Jesuit Social Services reach out into the world to influence hearts and minds to build a just society – we do this through our services, education, advocacy, capacity building and leadership development. The leaves reflect the fruits of our efforts, providing shade, colour and beauty. And through it all is the sap, the life force flowing from our roots (i.e., our spiritual foundations, our heritage, our founding story) through the trunk and branches to the leaves and beyond.

That is a symbolic way to understand how the mission is the foundation and roots, and the life force that inspires, informs, shapes and sustains the whole organism. Symbols are important, but they only work if behind them is something of substance, something true.

For us at Jesuit Social Services these foundations or roots include Ignatian spirituality (St Ignatius of Loyola was the founder of the Jesuits), the Jesuit justice tradition and Catholic Social Teaching. It is important for the leaders to have a deep knowledge of these roots, because it is their job to 'read and interpret' them for the current time and context. They need to be able to tell the story, to make it contemporary, accessible and useful *now*. There is no point in simply relaying a 'dead' story – we need to think of who our people are, the society from which they come, namely a pluralist, secular society. It is our job to understand our own founding story (and all that goes with that) and to make it available, to invite people to come on board, not to impose it in a rigid way, but to engage with it ourselves and to invite others to engage with it also. It is critical in doing this, that our starting point is respect and a recognition that people do not come to us as 'blank slates'. They come with their own history and stories, values and commitment. They are not waiting to be 'filled up' with our story but, if engaged respectfully, my experience is that they are more than willing to engage with and contribute to our unfolding story, to make it richer.

But the leader's job is more than this – there is a 'double' translation that needs to occur. First, there is the fundamental translation of the founding story, about which I have just written, and then the translation or application of that story to our work.

One of the things that is often mentioned about St Ignatius is his conversion during his convalescence after he had a leg shattered by a cannon ball in a battle. This is fine as a biographical point but what is a 21st century person (likely one with a lapsed or no faith background) meant to make of it? Thus, a double translation or interpretation needs to occur. What is the relevance of this in our understanding of our founding story, and then what might the implications of this be for our work on the ground?

For us at Jesuit Social Services there is a rich spirituality and heritage from which to draw. In common, everyday language we name some of those things as:

- always having a starting point of gratitude;
- coming from a place that is world-affirming;
- the centrality of relationship and being in solidarity with the poor and marginalised;
- the importance of grounded experience as our starting point;
- living a faith that does justice by being prepared to speak the truth to those in power;

- advocating for justice;
- a commitment to go to the frontiers, to go where others will not or cannot go;
- seeking to do more, go further, go deeper;
- seeking the greater good, the universal good, where the effect of our work can be magnified.

We draw on the story of St Ignatius to underpin and shape the way we work, e.g., that he was a pilgrim. Further, he developed the framework for the Jesuit order such that its members were to be free to go, to move in response to need, to be universal, available and mobile. St Ignatius was also on about interior freedom – what are the unhealthy attachments that we have (and about which we perhaps have a blind spot) that mean we are not free, that mean we are 'stuck'?

In the day to day, we draw on this tradition, reflect on it when we are faced with new and emerging needs, when we get 'bogged down', when we are trying to discern next steps. Our Ignatian and Jesuit heritage provides us with some tools to help us deal with these blockages and to move from reflection to purposeful and strategic action. We need to bring these to bear in the present but also as we plan for the future so that we are free to consider and then to address unmet need, unpopular need, to go where others will not or cannot go, to let go of something good for the better.

We also draw on the principles of Catholic Social Teaching – human dignity, solidarity, the common good and subsidiarity – putting flesh on them as we tease out how they inform our choices, our decisions, our practice models.

So these are our roots and we work to bring them to life in Jesuit Social Services. Others have different roots, a different founding story, but I am sure that these also lend themselves to that double interpretation, first to our current context and then to their application in our actual work, our interventions, our practice. But where and how does this get played out in a Catholic social service?

I see it like this. It is not just in the work we do, our practice, even including how we do it. I think what we are striving for, in order to have mission actively embodied in the culture of the organisation, is *integrity*. I use that word with the meaning of 'integrity' as moral, ethical behaviour and also 'integrity' in the sense of unity, wholeness.

So we are striving for integrity across the various domains of the 'human spirit' of the people who make up the Jesuit Social Services community, the practice framework that ensures our services and influencing work are informed and effective, and the organisational or business processes that ensure our people and services are resourced, developed and accountable. These domains are the three sets of energies and systems which are the basis of our spirit and culture and that are brought together in the day-to-day life of Jesuit Social Services in what we call our way of proceeding (Figure 2).

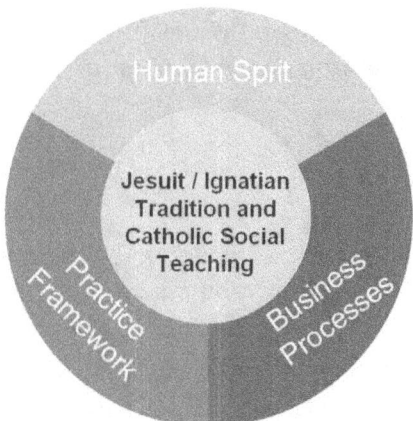

Figure 2: Jesuit Social Services' Way of Proceeding

Integrity across these domains shapes and expresses the spirit and culture of Jesuit Social Services. The systems and frameworks within these domains are typically articulated in policies and practices that reflect contemporary standards and expectations, and are further enhanced by being infused with the expression of Jesuit Social Services' unique Ignatian/Jesuit heritage. So we are striving for integrity both within and between these domains and in how they are played out at the personal, team and organisational levels.

The aim is to provide a line of sight between our current practices and our originating inspiration and heritage. So let us go back to our vision: Jesuit Social Services' vision is to build a just society. That is the thing on which we need to keep our eye, the thing that is our benchmark, the touchstone for all we do. Everything has to be tested against this. Is our behaviour contributing to this? Is the activity we are doing and how we are doing it contributing to this? Are our organisational processes – our human resource policies, the way we manage resources, investments – contributing to this? We have an Ignatian/Jesuit 'well' in the centre of all our activity on which we can draw (or, using the image of the tree, our roots) to facilitate good expression of our mission in each of these domains.

Human Spirit

So let us start with *human spirit*. First, what do I mean by the human spirit? I mean our very selves. I believe the most important asset we have is our people. It is people who will bring our mission to life, who are the arms and legs of the mission. In this work (and you could argue not just in this type of work, but it is particularly important in this work) it is imperative that we understand that our very person is the instrument we use: the painter has his brush, the surgeon her scalpel, but in our work we have ourselves. And so it is important that we keep refining ourselves, honing our skills, understanding what motivates us, pushes and pulls us, developing our capacity for self-reflection, for discernment, for relationship, for action.

The spirit has to do with a person's search for meaning: their desires, their sense of belonging, their self-giving, their being at peace with themselves. Spirit is also evident in building relationships, in openness to the 'other', and ultimately in openness to the transcendent. Importantly, spirit is part of bodily life, not separate from it.

Drawing on the wisdom of our Jesuit heritage, Jesuit Social Services seeks to develop the domain of the human spirit among our people and our works. Some of the capacities for which we recruit, then induct and support ongoing development are:

- a welcoming, generous, reflective and courageous attitude;
- being sensitive, respectful and attentive to the unique gifts, culture and circumstances of every person;
- a desire to help every person freely and fully to find their purpose and achieve their potential;
- a willingness to work collaboratively;
- the courage to stay with people, not to give up.

Central to our practices is the belief that staff are drawn to this work because of a vocational heart and the organisation is committed to nurturing this in our people. Our recruitment, induction, training and appraisal are key and formal processes in the development of the human spirit at Jesuit Social Services. We have numerous ways that we support this, for example we exercise our commitment to reflection in various ways such as beginning all our meetings across the organisation with a reflection where people get the opportunity to consider how their values and the values of the organisation are being lived out in their day-to-day practice.

Practice Framework

Now let us consider the domain of *practice framework*. This covers what we do: our core business, our interventions (our programs of support, our community college offering education and training, our social enterprises and employment pathways). It also includes our influencing-work, i.e., our advocacy; our capacity building activity; and our leadership development initiatives.

Our practice framework, in striving to be the best it can be, remains open to revision and renewal. St Ignatius challenged the Jesuits always to seek the most effective pathway in their work. He called this the *Magis*, a Latin word that means 'the more' or 'the greater'. He understood that this love shows itself in deeds rather than in words. In terms of practice, the *Magis* means to undertake the better choice, the more effective enterprise, the more influential option, and the work that meets the greatest need, because such a course, though probably harder, yields the greater good. It requires us to be more loving and so to contribute to the greater glory of God and the common good.

Our practice framework draws, of course, on good practice models and standards from, for example, social work, youth work, community development and psychology, informed by the latest research and literature, but it also draws on our heritage to inspire and to shape what we do and how we do it. Drawing on the fundamental principles of Catholic Social Teaching, for example the human dignity of each person and solidarity, and on our Ignatian tradition, we are encouraged to make our starting point people's actual experience. Then to reflect on that, to use our minds (what is the data telling us? the research? our discernment?), so our hearts and heads are always together for action in this tradition.

St Ignatius was not interested in just any kind of action but rather action that helped the person become more themselves, action that strengthened their values, their valuing of themselves and others. For St Ignatius it was imperative to be mindful of context – a person's, a community's. He spoke of "always being mindful of the circumstances of place and person" (so not having a one-size-fits-all solution to dealing with people and communities). Further, given that St Ignatius was a pilgrim, someone on the way to somewhere, he valued the process. Therefore in our engagement with people and communities, we draw on that to reinforce an approach that respects each person's unfolding story. We can only start where they are, respect that, accompany them, conscious that we are not the expert on another person's life.

In line with our Jesuit heritage, we have articulated our practice framework into our Way of Working, our core statements (like our vision, mission and values) and our guiding principles. Then we drill right down to the level of logics for each program, informed by evidence, our practice wisdom and our heritage.

Remembering that we are not solely in the business of delivering services, rather our goal is to build a just society by accompanying people to realise their full potential, the acronym is VALUE (Valuing, Affirming, Linking, Using, Enhancing) (Figure 3). Thus, whatever work we are doing with people and communities we are aware we are on a value pathway with them. It starts with relationship (nothing happens without that) but we then use that relationship to work with the person so they grow to valuing themselves and others. Many of the people with whom we work do not have any hopes or dreams; they do not think they have any skills. We work with them so they can develop and affirm their skills and aspirations and are able to link into support (this is the component that most people think of as what we do at Jesuit Social Services, but it is just one part of our way of working). We then provide opportunities for them to use, to practise their skills and capacities, and what we are aiming for is that they enhance their civic participation, take up their roles as valued and contributing citizens of our community, through training, volunteering or work.

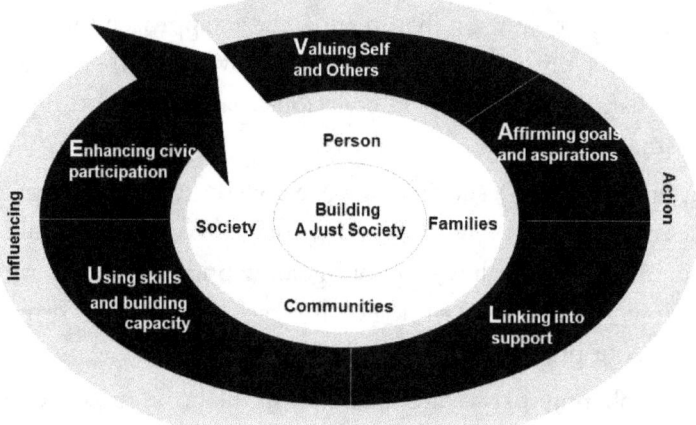

Figure 3: Jesuit Social Services' Way of Working

Our advocacy, capacity-building work and our leadership development activity all articulate with this. We draw on the Catholic Social Teaching principles of the common good and subsidiarity to inform our community work, e.g., in Aboriginal communities in Central Australia. And drawing on our Ignatian heritage, our advocacy always starts and is informed by grounded experience; it is relational, life-affirming, rigorous intellectually, and courageous as we are willing to speak the truth to those in power. So we draw on the 'well' of our roots to inform *how* we do what we do.

Business Processes

Then there is the third domain of *business processes*. These are concerned with the infrastructure that ensures that Jesuit Social Services are viable, efficient, accountable, transparent and appropriately resourced. They include areas such as governance, information technology, human resources, finance, communications, fundraising, property, risk management, environmental sustainability and procurement.

The Jesuit way of proceeding in what is called the "administration of temporal goods" is guided by the radical principle that these goods are to be regarded as the "patrimony of Christ's poor". Drawing on this, we appreciate that infrastructure exists for the effectiveness of the organisation, that people are more important than things, and that material resources ultimately are for the service of the poor and disadvantaged. This propels us to ensure that our infrastructure is efficient and effective. Resources are a gift to be responsibly managed and shared; sound investment and financial management are consistent with our work for a just society; in line with the principle of subsidiarity we encourage the appropriate level of decision-making; we are committed to sustainable practices and care of the environment, and to continuous evaluation of the effectiveness of our business processes to ensure their alignment with our vision, mission and values.

Conclusion

So in conclusion, let me put this approach together from our vision right through to our day-to-day practice. In Figure 4 the elements on the left-hand side are non-negotiable – we do not 'tamper' with foundations like human dignity but, over time and informed by the latest research and literature and our reflections on this along with our practice wisdom, we stay open to changing what we do and how we do it in order to achieve those foundational principles. Thus, our programs take on different shapes over time.

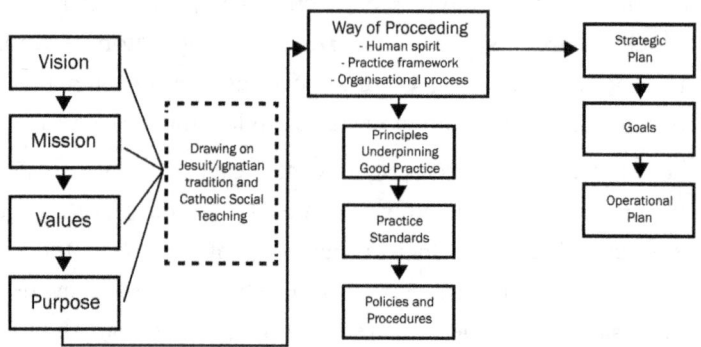

Figure 4: Jesuit Social Services' Approach: From Vision to Day-to-Day Practice

Returning finally to the image above of the tree – you see the roots, which are normally not seen but are, in fact, as deep and widespread as what is visible to the eye and without the roots the tree will not last. Those roots are our mission. They cannot be cut off or separated out to be the responsibility of one person, like the chief executive officer or the mission director. The mission is the foundation of the organisation and from it comes the agency's life force. It is everybody's business. Without it, we are like a tree without roots.

4

Catholics' Radical Alternative

Frank Brennan SJ

The hands and feet of Australian Church workers have reached into every corner of the country. We are a community of faith, formed and informed in the tradition of Catholic Social Teaching (CST). One of my ongoing formation communities is my extended family. I am blessed with 20 living nephews and nieces and my newest grandniece is number eight of that next generation. My oldest grandnephew is Liam aged six. His mother, one of my nieces, wrote the other day with news of Liam's latest school assignment at the local convent school. He was asked to use a computer to write the instructions he would give to an intending passenger who had never been on a train before. Liam just loves trains so the mechanical instructions were unsurprisingly very detailed. What did surprise me, and his mother, were the last two points: "After you've got home, tell yourself if you liked the journey; and, if you liked the journey, ring me. You might like trains as much as me." Reflection on experience and sharing the reflection on experience in community are constitutive for those of us who find that CST is continuing to shape our mission.

Chris Lowney tells the wonderful story of President Kennedy who meets the janitor at NASA and asks him what he does. The response: "I'm helping to put a man on the moon." And he was; and they all were. The NASA staff were working together on a common mission.

We are called to work together to facilitate the breaking in of the Kingdom here on earth. We all have our roles to play. Let us choose just one aspect of that mission. How is each of us helping to shape and implement an ethical, humane, compassionate national response to asylum seekers arriving on our shores by boat?

The language of CST must always be prophetic, pedagogical and practical. CST is not just words. It is reflected in words, actions and structures. One of the credibility problems for our Church today is that we proclaim a message of justice, inclusion and non-discrimination within a structure which is sexist and without sufficient theological coherence or scriptural warrant and which has been grossly neglectful of the best interests of the most vulnerable — abused children. CST provides us with ideas, feeds our imaginations, fires our passions, underpins our conversations, and animates our celebrations in relation to faith and justice — belief in a loving God and solidarity with our fellow human beings. Being Catholic, we respond as community, not as atomised individuals. Our responses are marked by service and ritual, informed by tradition and authority, as well as reflection on lived experience.

The last three popes have armed us with some wonderful concepts for taking on the task of shaping a world bearing more the marks of the Kingdom to come.

In his 1987 encyclical *Sollicitudo Rei Socialis*, Pope John Paul II spoke of the interdependence of the head and the solidarity of the heart. He told us:

> However much society worldwide shows signs of fragmentation, expressed in the conventional names First, Second, Third and even Fourth World, their interdependence remains close. When this interdependence is separated from its ethical requirements, it has disastrous consequences for

the weakest. Indeed, as a result of a sort of internal dynamic and under the impulse of mechanisms which can only be called perverse, this interdependence triggers negative effects even in the rich countries. It is precisely within these countries that one encounters, though on a lesser scale, the more specific manifestations of under-development. Thus it should be obvious that development either becomes shared in common by every part of the world or it undergoes a process of regression even in zones marked by constant progress. This tells us a great deal about the nature of authentic development: either all the nations of the world participate, or it will not be true development.[38]

Inviting us to move from the head to the heart, from thinking to taking a stand, Pope John Paul II then spoke of solidarity:

> At the same time, in a world divided and beset by every type of conflict, the conviction is growing of a radical interdependence and consequently of the need for a solidarity which will take up interdependence and transfer it to the moral plane. Today perhaps more than in the past, people are realizing that they are linked together by a common destiny, which is to be constructed together, if catastrophe for all is to be avoided. From the depth of anguish and fear …, the idea is slowly emerging that the good to which we are all called and the happiness to which we aspire cannot be obtained without an effort and commitment on the part of all, nobody excluded, and the consequent renouncing of personal selfishness.[39]

Pope Benedict XVI gave us useful insights into the relationship

---

38 Pope John Paul II, *Sollicitudo Rei Socialis*, 1987, section 17; accessed on 26 January 2014 at www.vatican.va.
39 Ibid., section 26.

between faith and politics in his encyclical *Deus Caritas Est*. He says:

> Justice is both the aim and the intrinsic criterion of all politics. Politics is more than a mere mechanism for defining the rules of public life: its origin and its goal are found in justice, which by its very nature has to do with ethics. The State must inevitably face the question of how justice can be achieved here and now. But this presupposes an even more radical question: what is justice? The problem is one of practical reason; but if reason is to be exercised properly, it must undergo constant purification, since it can never be completely free of the danger of a certain ethical blindness caused by the dazzling effect of power and special interests.[40]

Here politics and faith meet. Faith by its specific nature is an encounter with the living God – an encounter opening up new horizons extending beyond the sphere of reason. But it is also a purifying force for reason itself. From God's standpoint, faith liberates reason from its blind spots and therefore helps it to be ever more fully itself. Faith enables reason to do its work more effectively and to see its proper object more clearly. This is where Catholic social doctrine has its place: it has no intention of giving the Church power over the State. Even less is it an attempt to impose on those who do not share the faith, ways of thinking and modes of conduct proper to faith. Its aim is simply to help purify reason and to contribute, here and now, to the acknowledgment and attainment of what is just.

Pope Francis, anxious to demonstrate the continuity of CST, made few changes to Benedict's draft of what was to be his last encyclical and published *Lumen Fidei* as his own first encyclical. Francis speaks of the contemporary relevance of our faith for all people, helping

---

40 Pope Benedict XVI, Encyclical Letter, *Deus Caritas Est*, 2005, section 28; accessed on 26 January 2014 at vatican.va.

us to contribute to the common good: "Faith is truly a good for everyone; it is a common good. Its light does not simply brighten the interior of the Church, nor does it serve solely to build an eternal city in the hereafter; it helps us build our societies in such a way that they can journey towards hope."[41]

These concepts of interdependence and solidarity, the relationship between faith and politics, and the assurance that Christian faith can assist everyone committed to justice and the common good, can be harnessed prophetically, pedagogically and practically to formulate our proposals, actions and structures for a more just and peaceful world. They are the building blocks which come to life when we wrestle with a question such as how we might make our asylum policy more humane and more just.

During the 2013 federal election, we Australians were confronted with our major political parties trying to outbid each other with a 'shock and awe' campaign aimed at 'stopping the boats'. Some of us tried to be prophetic with our denunciations. Others pragmatically tried to temper the likely callous outcomes.

In terms of the short-term solution to the loss of life at sea and the expanding trade of the people smugglers luring increasing numbers of asylum seekers to Indonesia for transit to Australia, we all need to work within the reality that all major political parties in Australia are committed to a 'shock and awe' approach. Some of us are prepared to discuss how that 'shock and awe' approach might be tailored to be less callous and objectionable. Others find it so objectionable as to not warrant discussion. Many of us are just deeply troubled and have no idea what to do or say, hoping the problem will go away soon. If in the midst of the evil of the present situation, I can do something to

---

[41] Pope Francis, Encyclical Letter, *Lumen Fidei*, 2013, section 51; accessed on 26 January 2014 at vatican.va.

save one life or to accord proper protection to one additional refugee I will do it. I am very grateful that people schooled in CST have been prepared to engage in ongoing dialogue on this issue.

When confronted with moral evil in public policy, church personnel always have a choice: to be prophetic sticking to the moral absolutes (like the Greens or the US-style Right to Life Movement), or to be practical engaging in the compromises needed to temper the evil (like the major political parties and those who agitate better welfare measures for mothers so that they might be less likely to choose abortion). Whichever option we take, we all need to concede that at the moment, the only political parties not wanting to embrace a short-term 'shock and awe' approach are the Greens, the Democratic Labor Party and the Palmer United Party. I wish them all the best, but neither Christine Milne, John Madigan nor Clive Palmer, respectively, will ever be prime minister.

Given the large number of Catholics in the Abbott Cabinet, I hope they are listening and happy to contribute to the conversation with those of us who want to utilise CST prophetically, pedagogically and practically. It is great that we Catholics can have the conversation, anyone can contribute, and everyone can listen in.

Many of the Abbott Cabinet are Jesuit alumni. On the Jesuit *Eureka Street*[42] site there has been some spirited disagreement about the effects of a Jesuit education on our national decision makers. One alumnus, Dr John Frawley, said it was heartening to see Tony Abbott's education in a Jesuit school coming through. An ex-Jesuit Michael Breen found this too much:

> Do you mean the self-announced pragmatic opportunism, the callousness, the economy before people, the shallow

---

42 See eurekastreet.com.au.

thinking, the rank materialism, the slogans, the disregard for our international obligations, the ignorance of cultural and social matters, the blind eye to newcomers who can afford a plane fare? It is heartening to see the lesson in human compassion given him by Infidel Indonesian commentators which contrast with Abbott's Christian Values? No John, ever since Jesuit education has become the captive of their rich materialistic parent client body, don't expect too much of that New Testament stuff. I left the Jesuits for several reasons one of which is that I could not teach in a Jesuit school with a good conscience any more.

Dr Frawley spoke of other aspects of a Jesuit education:

> When my wife nearly died on us many years ago and left 7 children (aged 3-15) effectively motherless, 50 mothers from the Jesuits schools in Sydney came to the house every day for a year on a roster system to care for my wife, to teach her all the things she had forgotten and looked after the children so that I could go back to work. The Jesuit headmaster of Riverview took 6 boys into the boarding school and looked after them and refused to send me a bill. That, Michael, is what a Jesuit community is about to me and perhaps you can see why it saddens me that you seemingly could not find that Jesuit community in your experience. I genuinely hope that you will one day find it again.

Words, actions and structures have all played their part. During the 2013 election, the boys at Riverview of their own accord wrote to Tony Abbott and all the other Jesuit alumni in the major political parties: "We feel compelled to express our disappointment that, as graduates of our Jesuit schools, you would allow those principles, cultivated in our common tradition, to be betrayed. We look for heroes among our alumni, for insignes (generous and influential people, as St Ignatius styled them). Instead we see only allegiances to parties that trade human lives for political expediency, that choose the lowest common denominator to woo the populace, and that speak of economic problems rather than the dignity of the human person, especially the most vulnerable." This was highly prophetic language.

Riverview is a very different school from what it was in Tony Abbott's day. One structural difference is that there are now routine scholarships for Indigenous Australians and for refugees. So the life experience of the boys is different. Their reflection on their school experience is different. It was this difference that helped to motivate the boys of 2013 to write. The chief author of the letter told the media that the boys had been listening to the stories of their refugee mates: "Knowing first-hand the direct conflicts they have faced and seeing politicians making decisions that aren't taking into account humanity made us very upset. We wanted to evoke the feeling of what they experienced at Riverview and try to remind them that, when it comes right down to it, it's not about making decisions based on politics. It's about trying to come back to core values."

Tony Abbott has been receiving a number of letters from students educated in CST. Isabel Teixeira, a Year 12 student at Good Counsel College, Innisfail, and daughter of a Timorese refugee, wrote him a five page letter saying:

> If this proposed policy or even the current policy had been established and implemented when my father was seeking asylum from the war in Timor-Leste in the 1970s, I would not exist. However, they were not the policies of the 1970s and, as a result, my father was able to live in Australia, work as a member of parliament in both Australia and Timor-Leste, owns his own law firm and has educated his own children to understand the importance of human rights'

conservation. Is this not a gain for Australia? Mr Abbott, you know the facts, and if having them reiterated has still not evoked some form of recognition of the illegality of the policies, then I would like you to consider this: by you turning back these boats, carrying people who are potentially escaping situations which most Australians would consider nothing less than horrific, you are turning your back on any inkling of humanity which, through your actions, Australia maintains.

These prophetic utterances from young Catholics will not win the day on their own. But they are not useless. They are not simply romantic doodlings of out-of-touch do-gooders. Pope Francis has been very prophetic in his utterances on the same topic. The island Lampedusa is the European equivalent of our hellish Christmas Island. It is a lightning rod for European concerns about the security of borders in an increasingly globalised world where people as well as capital flow across porous borders. That is why Pope Francis went there on his first official papal visit outside Rome. At Lampedusa on 8 July 2013, Pope Francis said:

> Where is your brother? Who is responsible for this blood? In Spanish literature we have a comedy of Lope de Vega which tells how the people of the town of Fuente Ovejuna kill their governor because he is a tyrant. They do it in such a way that no one knows who the actual killer is. So when the royal judge asks: 'Who killed the governor?', they all reply: 'Fuente Ovejuna, sir'. Everybody and nobody! Today too, the question has to be asked: Who is responsible for the blood of these brothers and sisters of ours? Nobody! That is our answer: It isn't me; I don't have anything to do with it; it must be someone else, but certainly not me. Yet God is asking each of us: 'Where is the blood of your brother which

cries out to me?' Today no one in our world feels responsible; we have lost a sense of responsibility for our brothers and sisters. We have fallen into the hypocrisy of the priest and the Levite whom Jesus described in the parable of the Good Samaritan: we see our brother half dead on the side of the road, and perhaps we say to ourselves: 'poor soul ... !', and then go on our way. It's not our responsibility, and with that we feel reassured, assuaged. The culture of comfort, which makes us think only of ourselves, makes us insensitive to the cries of other people, makes us live in soap bubbles which, however lovely, are insubstantial; they offer a fleeting and empty illusion which results in indifference to others; indeed, it even leads to the globalisation of indifference. In this globalised world, we have fallen into globalised indifference. We have become used to the suffering of others: it doesn't affect me; it doesn't concern me; it's none of my business! Here we can think of Manzoni's character – 'the Unnamed'. The globalisation of indifference makes us all 'unnamed', responsible, yet nameless and faceless.[43]

Then on his recent visit to the Jesuit Church in Rome he said:

After Lampedusa and other places of arrival, our city, Rome, is the second stage for many people. Often – as we heard – it's a difficult, exhausting journey; what you face can even be violent – I'm thinking above all of the women, of mothers, who endure this to ensure a future for their children and the hope of a different life for themselves and their family. Rome should be the city that allows refugees to rediscover their humanity, to start smiling again. Instead, too often, here, as in other places, so many people who carry residence

---

43 Pope Francis, homily at Lampedusa on 8 July 2013; accessed on 26 January 2014 at vatican.va.

permits with the words 'international protection' on them are constrained to live in difficult, sometimes degrading, situations, without the possibility of building a life in dignity, of thinking of a new future!⁴⁴

Some of this sounds like politics! In one of his regular recent homilies, Francis made it clear that the gospel and politics do mix. Reflecting on the centurion who asked healing for his servant, Francis said that those who govern "have to love their people", because "a leader who doesn't love, cannot govern – at best they can discipline, they can give a little bit of order, but they can't govern". He mentioned "the two virtues of a leader" – love for the people and humility:

> You can't govern without loving the people and without humility! And every man, every woman who has to take up the service of government, must ask themselves two questions: 'Do I love my people in order to serve them better? Am I humble and do I listen to everybody, to diverse opinions in order to choose the best path.' If you don't ask those questions, your governance will not be good. The man or woman who governs – who loves his people is a humble man or woman.⁴⁵

Francis insisted that none of us can be indifferent to politics:

> None of us can say, 'I have nothing to do with this, they govern. . . .' No, no, I am responsible for their governance, and I have to do the best so that they govern well, and I have to do my best by participating in politics according to my ability. Politics, according to the Social Doctrine of the

---

44 Pope Francis, speech at Astalli Center, Rome on 10 September 2013; accessed on 26 January 2014 at jrseurope.org.
45 Pope Francis, homily on 16 September 2013; accessed on 26 January 2014 at en.radiovaticana.va.

> Church, is one of the highest forms of charity, because it serves the common good. I cannot wash my hands, eh? We all have to give something!

He then became a little playful in his homily:

> 'A good Catholic doesn't meddle in politics.' That's not true. That is not a good path. A good Catholic meddles in politics, offering the best of himself, so that those who govern can govern. But what is the best that we can offer to those who govern?

He concluded:

> So, we give the best of ourselves, our ideas, suggestions, the best, but above all the best is prayer. Let us pray for our leaders, that they might govern well, that they might advance our homeland, might lead our nation and even our world forward, for the sake of peace and of the common good.[46]

These prophetic remarks need to be matched by practical suggestions. We need to come to the table of practical deliberation committed to finding a better way to treat those who risk all on boats so that they might live. By forming and informing ourselves in CST we can contribute to a more just world prophetically, pedagogically and practically. Within the Church community we can sponsor the respectful dialogue needed so that the inevitable compromises of politics can be better tailored to justice for us all – acknowledging our interdependence and standing firm in solidarity.

---

46 Ibid.

PART TWO

Specific Questions

5

Are We There Yet?
Engagement with Aboriginal Communities

Vicki Clark and Peter Hudson

Prejudices are born out of ignorance and the only way to dispel ignorance is to have knowledge. The greatest knowledge is to have respect for every human being. (Vicki Clark)

With this reference to human dignity, which is a guiding principle of Catholic Social Teaching, this chapter begins its exploration of how Catholic community service organisations can build stronger collaborative relationships with our Aboriginal and Torres Strait Islander brothers and sisters. The guidance and articulation for this mutual journey comes from the landmark *Aboriginal Cultural Competence Framework* (ACCF) which was launched by the Victorian Government in November 2008 to guide mainstream Community Service Organisations (CSOs) in the development of management strategies, policies and direct practice which will provide better outcomes for Aboriginal children and families. The ACCF provides some very succinct and practical guidelines for CSOs. The definition of culture provided is enlightening and empowering:

> Culture, for Aboriginal peoples, enhances a deep sense of belonging and involves a spiritual and emotional relationship to the land that is unique ... For Aboriginal children, their families and communities, cultural competence is a means through which First Peoples can be given due respect and

honour in this their land and in the context of a history of racism and cultural abuse. Furthermore, it enables the broader community to understand the resilience and appreciate the pride Aboriginal peoples have about their culture. It also enables the broader community to celebrate and take pride in this the oldest continuing culture.[47]

In this paper we seek to overlay this description with the enduring and systematic implementation of the principles of Catholic Social Teaching (CST) by successive Popes in response to global and societal challenges of particular times in history. The key CST principles are human dignity, the common good, subsidiarity and solidarity.[48]

The ACCF counsels us that the process of developing collaborative relationships takes time. But it is essential that we pay heed to the warnings of Paulo Freire in reference to those of the dominant culture who seek to journey with marginalised people:

> It happens ... that as they cease to be exploiters or indifferent spectators or simply the heirs of exploitation and move to the side of the exploited, they almost always bring with them the marks of their origin [of being oppressors]: their prejudices and their deformations, which include a lack of confidence in the people's ability to think, to want and to know. Then a false solidarity emerges; one based on charity, paternalism or the desire for control.[49]

In other words, people from the dominant culture of a society who act to support marginalised people need to recognise that they

---

47 *Aboriginal Cultural Competency Framework* (ACCF), Victorian Government, 2008, p. 12.
48 Sandie Cornish, *How Catholic Social Teaching Can Help Us Respond to Issues*, Loyola Institute, Australian Jesuits, August 2006.
49 Paulo Freire, *Pedagogy of the Oppressed*, Penguin Books, Middlesex, 1972, pp. 36ff.

are still part of the dominant culture and so must take care that they do not 'speak for' or 'do for' the marginalised. Collaboration, therefore, requires that the partner from the dominant culture is aware of obvious and subtle power dynamics and continually seeks to walk alongside and not ahead of the marginalised partner.[50]

So, how are our agencies under the banner of Catholic Social Services meeting and responding to this challenge of cultural competency?

One important question to ask your organisation is the motivational one: Why do you want to engage with Aboriginal and Torres Strait Islander people? – is it because you need to tick the box, or is it because funding is available? Or is there a genuine commitment to engagement?

Protocols are an important part of all cultures and are in place to ensure people behave and interact in an appropriate manner. Observing the cultural protocols of a community demonstrates respect for the cultural traditions, history and diversity of that community. It also shows willingness to acknowledge that the processes and procedures of another cultural community are equally valid and worthy of the same respect as one's own cultural protocols.

Two examples of the challenges in building this mutual relationship follow. They summarise responses from professionals who attended the Catholic Social Services Victoria conference in October 2013 to the question, "What are your learnings as you journey with Aboriginal and Torres Strait Islander people?"

- **La Salle College, West Australia**

    Having 30+ remote community boarders in more recent years has been a rich learning experience for the whole

---
50 *ACCF*, op. cit., p. 30.

school community. Elders and families are welcomed regularly to the school for consultation and advice (e.g. on coping with the vast distances often associated with boarding, particularly at times of death within families). This commitment to Aboriginal and Torres Strait Islander students came out of the Principal's personal experience of involvement with the Balgo community.

- **Centacare Ballarat**

    A three-year period of relationship development with the Indigenous community in western Victoria has centred around Aboriginal and Torres Strait Islander families and seeking their opinion on what they feel will work for their community. It has been effective because of continuing conversations around "let's share what's working, what's not". There has been a gradual inclusion of Centacare staff in family events (e.g., funerals – a couple of years ago the staff would have been informed of a funeral, but more recently they have been invited along). The staff have discovered not to be afraid to ask questions respectfully. A big learning from this experience is that if you know the person's story, you will have a much greater chance of getting the 'protocols' right.

The challenge is to know the story which has historically been guarded by Aboriginal and Torres Strait Islander people. It is only recently, since the *Bringing Them Home* report was tabled in April 1997, that they have become more open to the possibility of counselling and importantly more culturally appropriate counselling services have been made available to Aboriginal and Torres Strait Islander peoples.

It is important to note that Aboriginal and Torres Strait Islander peoples, on many occasions, still feel judged by stereotypes before they enter into conversations with the non-Aboriginal people in main stream agencies. Unfortunately there are numerous negative stereotypes of Indigenous Australians, which are often perpetuated by the Australian media. These stereotypes can be damaging to relations between Indigenous and non-Indigenous Australians and often lead to acts of discrimination and racism.

It is very important to remember that there is enormous diversity amongst Aboriginal and Torres Strait Islander communities. These communities are made up of many different cultural groups, with different histories, languages, beliefs, opinions and traditions. Stereotypes are commonly based on ignorance and fear and have led to sweeping generalisations about Aboriginal and Torres Strait Islander people that are unfair and unfounded. Other stereotypes are to do with traditional images of Aboriginal Australia that are based in the past and fail to recognise that contemporary Aboriginal Australia is alive and well. Listed below are some of the more common stereotypes experienced by Aboriginal and Torres Strait Islander Australians. When working with their communities it is important to be aware of these stereotypes and to challenge them wherever possible:

- All Aboriginal and Torres Strait Islander people are welfare-dependent, or abuse alcohol and drugs.
- Aboriginal and Torres Strait Islander people of mixed descent are not 'truly' Aboriginal and Torres Strait Islander.
- All Aboriginal and Torres Strait Islander people will know or have heard of another Aboriginal or Torres Strait Islander person, or are experts on everything to do with Aboriginal culture.
- Aboriginal and Torres Strait Islander people do not want to work.
- Aboriginal and Torres Strait Islander people commit crime.

- Too much money is spent on Aboriginal and Torres Strait Islander affairs.
- Only Aboriginal and Torres Strait Islander people who choose to live in traditional societies are 'truly' Aboriginal and Torres Strait Islander.

It is important to remember that vulnerable mental health of Aboriginal and Torres Strait Islander peoples is very prevalent but still quite neglected. The following quote from *Bringing Them Home* describes this situation well:

> Issues relating to socio-cultural determinants, historical and political events, racism, cultural genocide and communal self-worth all impact on the scope of Aboriginal 'mental health'. The area of Aboriginal mental health is poorly understood; few experts would claim to fully understand the normal Aboriginal psyche or to confidently diagnose deviations ... Many of the so called mental health issues in the Aboriginal Community result from striving to fulfil the expectations of two different cultures – about finding a sense of place (South Australian Government final submission, page 54).[51]

"When you see a flag (Aboriginal and Torres Strait Islander), you know there's a battle that's been won". (Richard Franklin)

Catholic Social Services agencies should ask themselves the following: What signs and symbols do you have in your centres by way of welcome? What is behind the signs and symbols? Is there a commitment by the agency to the allocation of resources – personnel and financial – to shifting the culture?

It is very important to have Aboriginal and Torres Strait Islander

---

51 *Bringing Them Home*, Chapter 18, Mental Health Services, National Inquiry into the Separation of Aboriginal and Torres Strait Islander Children from Their Families, Commonwealth of Australia, 1997.

presence in many workplace conversations because this will greatly decrease the feeling of Aboriginal and Torres Strait Islander people being judged. There is still a lot of work to do to ensure that whoever walks through the door of a Catholic Social Services agency does not feel they are being judged. Importantly, when Aboriginal and Torres Strait Islander people enter an agency they need to see that the agency is on their side through appropriate signs and symbols.

If an Aboriginal or Torres Strait Islander person can speak to a fellow Indigenous Australian in the agency that immediately puts them at ease. More agencies need to employ Aboriginal and Torres Strait Islander workers. Having an Indigenous Australian involved in the decision-making gives an agency greater confidence to initiate partnerships which, of course, leads to more intensive engagement with the Aboriginal and Torres Strait Islander community. One of the critical issues around the employment of Aboriginal and Torres Strait Islander people is the professional qualification required to fill positions, which may deter them from applying. Potential applicants often have a lot of relevant experience but not always the qualification and this needs to be recognised by agencies when recruiting.

Catholic agencies also need to engage with the reconciliation issue much more actively and positively. There is no substitute for knowing the community with which you are working. Some agencies are doing the following:

- CatholicCare Sandhurst has successfully introduced effective messages and symbols and embarked on extensive cultural competency training and there also is the recognition that the initial training should be followed up regularly and creatively.
- Agencies need to keep a lookout for different groups of Indigenous Australians with similar needs/interests and

bring them together for the benefits of greater networking and cultural sensitivity.
- MacKillop Family Services is currently offering three traineeships for Aboriginal and Torres Strait Islander youth in administrative types of roles. It is a well-supported program with on-the-job training and regular specific mentoring.
- Many agencies could more specifically invite Aboriginal and Torres Strait Islander people to apply for positions through their advertising.

The following key principles should underpin all community consultation processes involving Aboriginal and Torres Strait Islander communities:

Respect Culture and Heritage – Be respectful of cultural protocols and practices and seek advice from community leaders.

Recognise Community Structures – Identify community leaders and organisations, and research the best method for communicating with them. One organisation does not represent the interests of the entire community.

Build Trust and Honour Commitments – It is important to remember that many Aboriginal and Torres Strait Islander communities have been deeply affected by the inappropriate policies and practices of past governments. For this reason it is essential to take the time to build long-term relationships with each community. These relationships must be based on trust, respect and honesty. It is very important to honour any commitments made to the community, and to find appropriate consultation mechanisms that ensure an open dialogue exists between the community and your agency.

The key messages that consistently emerge from the *Aboriginal Cultural Competency Framework* are:

- Cultural competence needs to be built over time, not overnight.
- Cultural competence requires a whole-of-agency approach and strong and committed leadership at all levels.
- Cultural competence relies on respectful partnerships with Aboriginal organisations and families.
- Cultural competence requires personal and organisational reflection.
- Cultural competence is a journey, not a destination.
- You are not expected to know it all![52]

So many of the elements of these messages echo the application of Catholic Social Teaching principles in the Catholic Church's continuing quest to discern "the signs of the times"[53] within the world at particular points in history and particularly within evolving cross-cultural societies. It is all about being faithful to the Gospel values of justice, equity and love of our neighbour. It must not be lip-service but a concrete commitment to building together a better world for everyone.

---

52 *ACCF*, op. cit., p. 54.
53 Pope John XXIII, Encyclical, *Pacem in Terris*, 1963, section 126; accessed on 26 January 2014 at vatican.va.

6

At the Crossroads: The Challenges of Child Sexual Abuse to Mission and Identity

Jenny Glare[54]

As the Church confronts the sexual abuse crisis, this is a critical time for providers of Catholic social services in Australia to reflect on what this means for us as individuals and as leaders of our organisations. We are 'at the crossroads' as we seek to address the challenges of child sexual abuse for our mission and identity.

Former Prime Minister Julia Gillard offered current Prime Minister Tony Abbott the following advice in her address at the Sydney Opera House of 30 September 2013. She said: "It is big step from criticising what you think is wrong to working out and implementing what you think is right." In our view, this advice has a place in our deliberations 'at the crossroads'.

Being 'at the crossroads' implies that we have to choose a direction in which to go. We must go on but which way? To the left, or to the right, or straight ahead? We cannot go backwards but neither can we completely ignore the images in our rear-view mirror. The past always contains lessons for the future.

We need to learn from the consequences of the devastating harm

---

54 The author gratefully acknowledges the contribution of Micaela Cronin to the development of this chapter and Ché Stockley for research assistance.

caused to those individuals who were entrusted to the care of Church organisations and who experienced sexual abuse. This means we must examine the policies and practices that operated in the past.

Ensuring that the children in our care today are safe from sexual abuse means that we must be vigilant in our choice of staff, have ongoing programs in place for supervision and monitoring, and create an organisational culture that is 'child-safe'.

Just as we must focus on healing for the individual, this also applies to our organisations. Our structures need to heal as well. The wounds in our shared story of sexual abuse are deep; cracks and fissures may still exist in our organisations today.

This work is hard and challenging but it is through these cracks and fissures that the light gets in and we find a way forward and there is hope for the future.[55]

The broad questions in moving forward, considered in this chapter, are:

- to whom do we listen?
- how do we learn?, and
- where do we find inspirational leadership?

The challenges of sexual abuse to our mission and identity can be summarised as follows:

- potential loss of credibility and reputation;
- understanding the shadow side of our organisational history;
- making our organisations safe for children in our care; and
- responding to disclosures of historical abuse.

---

[55] Leonard Cohen's *Anthem* from his album *The Future,* Columbia Records, 1992, includes the following text: "There is a crack, a crack in everything. That's how the light gets in."

Examples of some of the practices that one agency, MacKillop Family Services, has implemented to respond to these challenges are:

- providing mechanisms for complaints and feedback,
- understanding the ongoing trauma of sexual abuse,
- improved quality and standards frameworks, and
- developing cultural competence across the organisation.

In expanding on the above points, this chapter reviews MacKillop Family Services' journey since its formation, and looks at what we have learned and are still learning.

Introduction to MacKillop Family Services

More than 150 years ago the Christian Brothers, the Sisters of Mercy and the Sisters of St Joseph commenced their work in Victoria. Inspired by the charism of their founders, Edmund Rice, Catherine McAuley and Mary MacKillop, the three congregations established homes for children who were orphaned, destitute or neglected and homes for mothers who were in need of care and support.

Over time, the original model of institutional care evolved into different forms of residential care, foster care, education and family support services. In 1997 MacKillop Family Services (MacKillop) was formed, as a refounding of the earlier works, to provide a range of integrated services for children, young people and families.[56]

The new organisation operated in its first few months against a backdrop of media interest in abuse that had occurred in the old care institutions. *The Age* newspaper, for example, undertook a campaign to raise awareness of past abuse in children's homes in Victoria. *The Age* chose a different children's home as its focus each week. The

---

56 For further details, see mackillop.org.au – accessed on 4 January 2014.

stories were often accompanied by a photograph of adults standing in front of the home in which they grew up. Stories of abuse and neglect emerged from each home. For the new MacKillop, this was not the beginning for which we had hoped; it was more a baptism of fire.

Partly because of public scrutiny, but also thanks to the new organisation's belief in the rights of former residents, we made a commitment to offer a special program for men and women who had experienced childhood care and for mothers who had stayed at the previous care institutions. MacKillop believed that those who had grown up in these homes and orphanages should be able to access their own records with minimum constraints and with as much support as they needed. The Heritage and Information Service, developed to support this work, was a core MacKillop program from the beginning.[57]

MacKillop's founding board and management also recognised that the refounded organisation had much to learn from recollections and experiences of previous generations who had lived in institutional care and/or had been separated from their families of origin. Thus, the Heritage and Information Service was established within the first six months of launching the new organisation to ensure that the thousands of personal and organisational stories that came into MacKillop were not lost but preserved for the future. In our view, the original aims of "preserving the record, remembering the stories, connecting people and learning for today" still hold true, and it is hoped that anyone with a connection to our founding agencies might be able to find their individual or family story.

---

57 For further details, see mackillop.org.au/HeritageService – accessed on 4 January 2014.

MacKillop Family Services Today

The circumstances that led to the founding of MacKillop, the amalgamation of the child, youth and family work of the three Catholic religious congregations, gave rise to its unique identity amongst Catholic service social providers. As Neil Ormerod in his paper, "Identity and Mission in Catholic Organisations", states "Church-based agencies share, in some manner, the identity and mission of the Church. They may do so in different ways with different emphasis".[58] Ormerod provides a model for analysing mission and identity of organisations in terms of their religious, moral, cultural and social dimensions. He argues that organisations that work in the areas of health and welfare have a focus on the social, cultural and moral aspects of mission and identity of the Church.

MacKillop is now a leading provider of services for children, young people and their families in Melbourne, Geelong, Warrnambool, western Sydney and the south coast of New South Wales and we have recently expanded into Perth, Western Australia. The programs we deliver include foster care and residential care, disability services, youth support, education and training, family support, and refugee services. The Heritage and Information Service continues to provide support to women and men who, as children, were in the care of our founding agencies.

Most of the work we do today at MacKillop is funded by state and federal governments. As such, we are accountable to them for the services we provide, alongside our accountability to our clients, staff and Board. MacKillop is outward-focussed in the work we undertake and our accountabilities. The services were intended to be, and

---

58 Neil Ormerod, "Identity and Mission in Catholic Organisations", *The Australasian Catholic Record*, 2010, 87(4), pp. 430-439; see p. 431.

remain, independent from, but strongly connected to, our founding congregations. MacKillop's work is guided by our values:

- justice,
- hope,
- collaboration,
- compassion, and
- respect.

Challenges for MacKillop Family Services

Potential Loss of Credibility and Reputation

Like other Catholic social services today, MacKillop has been challenged by the disclosures of sexual abuse at all levels of the Church and in organisations connected to the Church. We have increasingly become aware of a system of caring for children that failed to prevent the abuse of children, and then tried to cover up or deny the existence of abuse. Some would argue that many of the institutions of the Church are still failing to deal with the long-term consequences of the abuse. In responding to this challenge some organisations will choose to distance their work from the Church and/or re-model their mission and identity, while others will embrace the task of addressing the challenges in the system.

As with other Catholic organisations, especially those that grew out of religious congregations, MacKillop is no longer staffed by members of religious congregations and primarily practising Catholics. What is relevant is that the organisation is very clear about where it stands in terms of its mission and there is an invitation to all staff who join the organisation to embrace its values and culture. The organisation practices inclusiveness and embraces diversity.

MacKillop's obligations to the children currently in our care, and the adults who were in care as children, have been bought into sharp focus by the Victorian Parliamentary Inquiry into the Handling of Child Abuse by Religious and Other Organisations and the Royal Commission into Institutional Responses to Child Sexual Abuse. Just as the Inquiry and the Royal Commission have illustrated the importance of 'bearing witness' to the experience of abuse, as the Commission itself is required to do as part of its terms of reference, this is also the case for the Church and Catholic services across Australia.

The Victorian Parliamentary Inquiry and the Royal Commission can be viewed as the latest in a series of historically significant systemic investigations into how children who entered the out-of-home care system have been and are cared for in Australia. Examples include the Senate inquiries into Children in Institutional Care, and Lost Innocents relating to child migrants. There was also the Australian Human Rights Commission's inquiry into the Stolen Generations, which led to the *Bringing Them Home* report. Other inquiries in Australia that are relevant include the current New South Wales Special Commission of Inquiry Concerning the Investigation of Certain Child Sexual Abuse Allegations in the Hunter Region, Queensland's 1999 Forde inquiry into the treatment of children in licensed government and non-government institutions, and similar inquiries in other states of Australia.

These inquiries have led, in turn, to apologies to the Stolen Generations in 2008 and to Forgotten Australians in 2009, and for forced adoption practices in 2013.

Notwithstanding the events unfolding in Australia, we need to remember that there have been similar inquiries in Britain, Canada, Ireland and the United States of America. In a way these inquiries have been like a portent of what is to come, so in a sense we should have been prepared. Experts and the Royal Commission itself, however, have warned that the stories that will be shared will generate disbelief, outrage and anger across the nation and for the Church.

Understanding the Shadow Side of Our Organisational History

Some Catholic institutions have not dealt well with the abuse and trauma of those in their care. Those who experienced abuse prior to coming into care were sometimes mistakenly regarded as 'damaged goods', therefore justifying abuse that occurred while in care. Those who complained of violence and abuse while in care were not believed, silenced, told they were dirty, or blamed. As adults, some have focused on survival and, when individuals have tried to return to the Church in an attempt to deal with the unfinished business of their childhood, their approach has been aggressively rebuked or passively brushed aside.

The Victorian Parliamentary Inquiry and the Royal Commission have shown that some Catholic institutions sought to minimise the impact of the abuse that occurred within their institutions, and their response was inadequate.

Many victims were surprised by the demeanour or statements of some witnesses at the Victorian Parliamentary Inquiry. An example of this was a senior Church leader's poor choice of words, when he used the phrase "better late than never" to refer to the time it took to seek laicisation of convicted sex offender Des Gannon. Whatever the intent, these words have continued to be viewed negatively by victims of clerical abuse.

In the view of many victims, statements like this go to a lack of preparedness to acknowledge the pain of the abuse they experienced, and to walk alongside those who have experienced abuse. The public perception of Church leaders is diminished when it seems as though they just do not 'get' the ongoing and devastating consequences of childhood abuse.

Indeed, the Chair of the Royal Commission, Peter McLellan, has acknowledged his own lack of understanding of abuse, even as a judge who has presided over many abuse cases. Thus, he stated recently:

> Although the impact on the lives of abused persons has been reported within the academic literature I have no doubt that it is not well understood by the general community. In my role as a judge I have been called upon to review many of the sentences imposed upon people convicted of the sexual abuse of children but I readily acknowledge that, until I began my work with the Commission, I did not adequately appreciate the devastating and long lasting effect which abuse can have on an individual's life.[59]

There is strength in acknowledging the limits of our knowledge and in a preparedness to understand the impact of abuse.

Making Our Organisations Safe for Children in Our Care

A significant factor in responding to the failings of the past is to ensure that present-day services for the children in our care are safe. MacKillop is of the view that a suite of organisational practices should be in place to ensure the safety of children. These include pre-employment screening, thorough interviewing, and reference and police checks. Ideally, these measures sit alongside good supervision practices and robust frameworks for responding to allegations of improper conduct or abuse.

Our services must also be nurturing. One of the themes that

---

59 Peter McLellan, Chair, Royal Commission into Institutional Responses to Child Sexual Abuse in a speech to Bravehearts White Balloon Day on 6 September 2013; accessed on 10 September 2013 at childabuseroyalcommission.gov.au/bravehearts-white-balloon-day-brisbane.

predominates in dialogue with adults who grew up in the previous era of children's homes is the harshness of the experience, and the absence of emotional warmth and positive encouragement. In an effort to create safe and healing environments for children, families and adults who have experienced chronic stress and adversity, MacKillop has introduced the Sanctuary model across the whole organisation as our model of care.[60] The Sanctuary model is a trauma-informed method for creating a culture of hope and innovation in agencies working with vulnerable people. The theoretical foundations of the Sanctuary model are drawn from trauma and attachment theory, business and systems theory, and therapeutic practice approaches.

With this initiative, we demonstrate that we are open to hearing from our clients about their experience of our services. We are committed to listening to the voices of the children in our care today but also of those adults who were in care in past eras. We are attuned also to listening for the unexpected and learning from what we hear.

Responding to Disclosures of Historical Abuse

It takes courage and a steadfast commitment to look at the practices of the past through the lens of those who were the recipients of the care provided rather than only from the standpoint of the providers of the service. Taking this view means listening with the heart, being open to other people's life stories, and listening for the unexpected. It also means being aware of the potential for hearing stories of abuse, and facing up to the unintended consequences of well-intentioned actions.

Through our work at the MacKillop Heritage and Information Service, we have learned much about the legacy of growing up in institutional care, and about the separation of children from their

---

[60] MacKillop is moving to become a registered Sanctuary organisation; see mackillop.org.au – accessed on 4 January 2014.

families, the separation of brothers and sisters from each other, and parents from their children. We have also come to appreciate the perspective of mothers separated from their babies through the practice of forced adoption. And we have become experienced also in hearing disclosures of abuse and learning of the ongoing trauma experienced across the life cycle for people who experienced childhood abuse.

Our work in supported release of records has confirmed that, whilst there is still much unfinished business to complete, there is much that is achievable. In July this year, we were proud to open the doors of our Heritage Centre for the first time. Together with the client records and the collection of artefacts, objects and memorabilia held in the Heritage Centre, we attempt to portray the experiences of our former residents, alongside the story of the religious congregations who provided the care. We value and re-tell the stories of our former residents as, in our view, they are important and have much to teach us, to inform our practice today.

Importantly, MacKillop continues to provide support and care to those who experienced abuse before they came into our care, while in our care and after leaving our care. For example, MacKillop has now hosted two events at the time of national apologies. On both occasions, people sat quietly and listened carefully to the words of the respective Prime Minister and Leader of the Opposition. The only sound was barely audible crying. The live screening of the apology was followed by lunch where many heartfelt gestures of comforting each other were observed. The mood was respectful and the apology was received with gratitude. Our practice of inviting former residents to watch these events live and share the experience with others demonstrates our preparedness to acknowledge the ongoing pain and suffering of our former residents.

We think that the establishment and continued support of the Heritage and Information Service, as a central element of MacKillop's work, signifies that the experiences of the children in the care of our founding agencies are a very real and present part of the work we do today. We do not view our history as something that took place 'back then'. Our heritage work encourages MacKillop staff today to think about how our services impact across time on the people in our care. Our founding congregations have been very supportive of the ongoing work of this service.

Exemplary Practices of MacKillop Family Services

Providing Mechanisms for Complaints and Feedback

MacKillop ensures that clients have the opportunity to provide feedback on their experience of our services. Staff are also frequently given the opportunity to provide feedback through staff satisfaction surveys and through surveys on discreet issues, such as management supervision practices.

In 2012 we undertook a survey involving all clients in recognition of two of the Sanctuary model's core principles: democracy and open communication. The benefits of asking clients what they think of our services, and being prepared to hear what they have to say, include the capacity to improve service delivery, building knowledge amongst staff and management about how our services are perceived, and client empowerment through the opportunity to give feedback and have a say in the services clients access. We were very pleased with the response rate across the organisation, and gained helpful insights from the input of those who use our services, with much of the feedback very positive. Subsequently, each operational area was provided with a summary of results to assist it in planning and service improvement.

Understanding the Ongoing Trauma of Sexual Abuse

MacKillop's implementation of the Sanctuary model is our attempt to understand trauma and equip our staff to create a safe and nurturing environment. The Sanctuary model is a targetted means to respond to the trauma which has been experienced by the children and adults who use our services, and also to acknowledge organisational trauma – the culture and practices that can go unrecognised and perpetuate unsafe workplaces.

Some would argue that the Church's response to claims of abuse in recent years arises from a fundamental lack of understanding about the long-lasting and devastating effects of abuse on children and young people. Through the Sanctuary model, MacKillop is learning to ask not "what is wrong with you?" but instead "what happened to you?".

The model is a blueprint for clinical and organisational change which, at its core, promotes safety and recovery from adversity through the active creation of a trauma-informed community. A recognition that adversity is pervasive in the experience of human beings forms the basis for the Sanctuary model's focus not only on the people who seek services, but equally on the people and systems providing those services.

In an effort to create safe and healing environments for children, families and adults who have experienced chronic stress and adversity, the Sanctuary model is employed across a wide range of settings.

Improved Quality and Standards Frameworks

Today, there is more scrutiny, quite rightly, of the care provided to children and young people than ever before. This is true of all community services. Additionally, it is MacKillop's responsibility, and a reflection of its mission and values, to monitor continually all the systems we have in place to ensure that they are still useful and meeting the changing needs of the organisation and service users. Quality Improvement refers to actions taken throughout an organisation to increase the effectiveness of activities and processes, and to provide added benefits to both the organisation and its clients.

Strategies employed by the MacKillop Quality and Compliance team to enhance quality include:

- communication and information provision to staff and carers,
- resourcing and participating in cross-organisational forums and working groups,
- supporting the development and review of practice manuals, procedures and documentation.

Most MacKillop programs are subject to external standards or requirements of funding bodies. MacKillop is committed to meeting all requirements of the legislative bodies in the states where it operates, as well as compliance requirements of the bodies that fund our services. Our reliance on government funding, as compared with donor funds, means we are particularly accountable to our funding bodies for the safety of our clients.

In our Victorian services, when quality of care complaints are made in relation to the children and young people in our care, the Department of Human Services (DHS) provides a comprehensive framework for their investigation and potential improvement of standards of care. DHS takes a lead role in the investigation of allegations of abuse and other quality of care concerns in the out-of-home care sector, including within MacKillop. Similar procedures are followed in our services in New South Wales and Western Australia.

MacKillop has policies in place to ensure we respond to allegations or instances of abuse in a transparent, timely, confidential and just manner. The best interests of the child or young person involved are at the centre of our practice.

Developing Cultural Competence Across the Organisation

Building cultural competence within an organisation is also a critical component of the organisational changes required to move forward. Cultural competence helps us to understand the context in which we operate, and allows us to work effectively within our communities, through acknowledging and valuing cultural diversity. Two relevant examples are MacKillop's Iftar dinner and the Koori Youth Traineeship program.

The annual Iftar dinner is hosted by MacKillop through its Family Relationship Centre in Broadmeadows. The dinner aims to build links and connections and, above all, a better understanding and appreciation of a cultural practice of a significant section of our society. The annual dinner, now in its fifth year, brings together senior MacKillop staff, key Muslim community representatives and people from about 60 different cultural, religious and ethnic groups.

The Koori Youth Trainee program is a new partnership between MacKillop and the Victorian Aboriginal Child Care Agency (VACCA) with the support of Kangan TAFE. The program gives trainees an opportunity to learn key work skills and gain experience in both an Aboriginal and a mainstream organisation. The traineeship is an initiative designed to develop, strengthen and improve outcomes when working with Aboriginal people within the community, and to deepen our cultural competence more broadly. We are hopeful that trainees will take up the opportunity of employment with VACCA or MacKillop at the end of the program.

Conclusion

It has been our experience that, although many senior leaders in the Church and other relevant agencies think they are responding appropriately to issues of abuse, the people with whom we work do not always feel that this is true for them. Victims' voices are often silenced in processes that are intended to support them and to provide redress for past harms.

MacKillop, as a Catholic service provider, has shown leadership in responding to abuse effectively. It has strived to advance understanding of what it means to be traumatised, and, as an organisation, we acknowledge the range of needs a person may have on their journey to healing.

This chapter illustrates, by means of the MacKillop case study, that faith-based organisations, including Catholic institutions, can learn from past mistakes and implement practical reforms. MacKillop is engaged in a number of projects which encourage us to 'bear witness' to the suffering of members of our community, but also to ensure that we are responding appropriately to their needs, with their interests at the centre of what we seek to do.

7

Engaging, Exploring and Enabling: Lessons in Executive Leadership from the Gospel of John

Julie Morgan

Contemporary leadership in Catholic organisations often draws its inspiration from the Scriptures. We are familiar with the passages in which Jesus, at his subversive best, deconstructs leadership and introduces the disciples and each of us to the notion that the person who wants to be a leader must first be a servant.[61] He is explicit and unequivocal that leadership is built on service.

The model of service that Jesus uses on the night before he dies has previously been offered to him by Mary, the sister of Lazarus, anointing his feet and then drying them with her hair and thereby connecting with him deeply and with extraordinary intimacy (*John* 12: 1–8; *Holy Bible: New Revised Standard Version*). She demonstrates a kind of service that is not passive or hesitant. On the contrary, it offers leadership, it is earthy and real, and it is utterly driven by passion. But if this is what servant leadership looks like, how is it enabled, and how does such leadership become transformational?

In one of the opening chapters in John's Gospel we are told about the encounter between Jesus and the unnamed woman at the well

---

61 Brian Yanofchick, "Servant Leadership: Bring It Home", *Health Progress*, Sept-Oct 2007, pp. 6-7.

(*John* 4). In this passage, we are offered some extraordinary insights into leadership that could provide Catholic organisations with a unique framework for nurturing organisational change.

The encounter begins with Jesus going through a Samaritan town called Sychar. He rests by the well in the heat of the noonday sun. One of the women from the town comes to the well to draw water for the day. The fact that she is there in the middle of the day, when all the other women of the village would have collected their water at sunrise, is an important clue given to us by the writer of John's Gospel; we begin to surmise that the woman is marginalised and isolated from her community. This realisation is pivotal to understanding the spectacular nature of what is about to unfold.

Engaging People

Jesus asks the woman for a drink of water; it is a rather blunt, almost rude demand. Yet it leads to an engagement initiated by Jesus and sustained by the woman that is quite extraordinary. She names the differences that lay between them, differences that should preclude relationship, that are incompatible with hospitality. Yet Jesus engages with her and continues the conversation. There is something about stopping on his journey in this hostile place, something about her that captivates him and that enables him to draw deeply on his sense of self. It is in this moment of authentic engagement that Jesus articulates something about *his* identity that has not been revealed before and will not be revealed again in the Gospels – that he is living water. What an extraordinary insight – that identity is discovered and articulated in the context of mission, of journey, of engagement with the least expected person.

Exploring Possibilities

The exchange between Jesus and the woman at the well quickly moves to the exploration of other possibilities. The woman hears what Jesus is saying at one level: "Sir, give me this water so that I may never be thirsty again or have to keep coming here to draw water." We can imagine that she may have stopped herself from saying, 'and so I do not have to keep coming back here every day demonstrating how alone and rejected I am'. Unwittingly she provides Jesus with an opportunity to explore something about *her* identity. "Go, call your husband and come back." The conversation moves rapidly and, for the woman at least, into dangerous territory: she has loved and lost many times. Clearly she has experienced betrayal and abandonment and no doubt she has been the cause of heartache, anger and despair. But her past – and her present – are explored within a conversation that is elicitive and accepting rather than judgmental. Despite all that has happened to her to make her suspicious of men, of outsiders, of anyone, there is something about him that engenders trust. In this encounter, nothing is closed down. Rather, everything is possible. Something powerful is happening in Jesus *and* in the woman and will happen for others because of this most unlikely person and this most unexpected conversation. There should be an urgency for us in this realisation: the irregularity of life of the unnamed woman at the well is, paradoxically, both significant and of no significance whatsoever for Jesus. This realisation challenges, cajoles and emboldens those of us struggling to think about how we go about leading organisations where many people have decided for themselves – or have been told – that their manner of life is unacceptable and therefore feel themselves to be on the margins of the Church.

Enabling Passions

It is now clear to us that it is the sexual nature of her sins that has caused her social isolation and which has been the catalyst for this chance encounter with Jesus. We have come to accept, rather casually at times, that Jesus preferred to be with social outcasts but what happens next is a glimpse into the transformational.

The disciples return and the writer of John's Gospel tells us that they were surprised to see Jesus talking with a woman. And while the disciples were surprised, it is not hard to imagine that other people in the village may have been watching this exchange between the woman-that-they-thought-they-knew-so-well and the Jewish stranger, and thinking, 'here she goes again, husband number 7'. Despite the fact that the disciples say nothing, their very presence means that the moment with Jesus is broken, judgment returns to the air and she senses it. So she leaves her water jar and rushes back into the town. The writer of John's Gospel tells us that she returns to the very people who have scorned, condemned and marginalised her. She is, however, so transformed by this conversation with Jesus, she is so deeply empowered by the way that he has engaged her, by the reciprocal way that they have explored their identities, that she is enabled to forget the disciples; she is enabled to go back to the people who have rejected her: "Come and see a man who told me everything I have ever done!" And she brings others to faith in him: "Many Samaritans from that city believed in him because of the woman's testimony." Is it possible that this unnamed woman, this sexual sinner, is the first 'lay' missionary in John's Gospel? Her transformation is complete. And Jesus' deconstruction of everything that the disciples expect a leader of faith to be is just beginning.

The Leadership Context

The encounter between Jesus and the woman at the well is breathtaking – there is something about this woman that enables Jesus to reveal himself as living water; there is something about Jesus that enables the woman to leave the boundaries that life has placed on her and to bring others to faith in him. And all of this happens within the context of conversation. What are we to make of this insight as we try to understand ever more deeply what leadership in the contemporary context could look like? It is the conversation between the leader and the least expected person that opens up the possibilities of something more. It is the conversation between them, witnessed by dumbfounded others, that models a different way of being with people who are vulnerable and marginalised. It is in the context of conversation that they both experience the unlocking of a deeper life.

What we see in this Gospel passage is a framework for leaders who are interested in creating a welcoming environment, of demonstrating that everyone matters, of building on the strengths and capabilities of everyone in the organisation – especially of the least expected to contribute. It is a style of leadership that is transformational because it takes everyone seriously; it engages people where they are yet offers them new possibilities.

So often in our organisations we are baffled by some staff whom we see as intransigent and stubborn. Other staff seem convinced of their marginalisation and unworthiness. Still others yearn for recognition and acceptance, while a happy few get on with the job. Aware of frailty and of possibility, of fracture lines and of potential, the transformational leader wants to engage with staff in ways which will unlock energy and optimise the promise that it is inherent in good people working together for others.

A Framework for Change

How could we go about providing a working environment where conversations that bring about deep change are possible? One way of thinking about the 'how' of change, is to think about transformation or deep change coming about through *deep learning*.

We learn every day, and much of this kind of learning is instrumental in that it helps us to do something. Sometimes we retain what we have learned and other times – as soon as its usefulness to us is over – we quickly forget it. But this sort of learning does not really change us. This is the kind of learning that happens in *training*.

Deep learning on the other hand occurs when 'old' or fixed knowledge, or 'old' or fixed attitudes or stances are no longer valid – they were meaningful once but they are no longer in alignment with the new or the deep insights that we have gained into ourselves, others and the world. Sometimes deep learning even takes place within the way that we think (and feel) about realities that we cannot see, touch, taste, smell and hear – experiences of transcendence like love, hope and our sense of who God is. What we have learned impacts on us deeply; it stays with us; it changes us from the inside and shapes new ways of living: perhaps we are gentler, more forgiving, more loving, more open, more secure in ourselves, more hopeful, more confident that despite the way that life disrupts our best laid plans, all will be well. This sort of deep change in us is quite often witnessed by others, especially those who know us well. Authentic change and transformation within the person are tangible in some way to those around us.

Thinking about transformation from a Catholic philosophical approach is provided by the Canadian Jesuit theologian Bernard Lonergan. He used the concept of *conversion* to imply the deep or radical shift that can take place in each of us as we encounter, absorb, wrestle with, and are transformed by what we experience and learn. Conversion can have pejorative connotations these days but, if we think about it as deep learning, we come closer to his insight about the dynamic ways in which we each develop and experience genuine growth. This kind of deep change within us is experienced within three horizons – the intellectual, the ethical and the spiritual. Lonergan speaks of such horizons in this way:

> In its literal sense the word, horizon, denotes the bounding circle, the line at which the earth and sky appear to meet. This line is the limit of one's field of vision. As one moves about, it recedes in front and closes in behind so that, for different standpoints, there are different horizons. Moreover, for each different standpoint and horizon, there are different divisions of the totality of visible objects. Beyond the horizon lie the objects that, at least for the moment, cannot be seen. Within the horizon lie the objects that can now be seen. As our field of vision, so too the scope of our knowledge, and the range of our interests are bounded. As fields of vision vary with one's standpoint, so too the scope of one's knowledge and the range of one's interests vary with the period in which one lives, one's social background and milieu, one's education and personal development.[62]

Transformational leaders are committed to enabling change – not forcing or mandating that everyone else in the organisation will change. They enable change by creating an environment where deep learning or deep change within all three horizons is made possible. This understanding of deep learning comes close to what many organisations are looking for when they talk about formative

---

62 Bernard J. Lonergan, *Method in Theology*, Toronto University Press, Toronto, 1973, pp. 235-236.

professional development for the staff and about executive education for the leaders. This kind of professional learning takes the whole person seriously, their head, their heart and their spirit. It is the kind of deep learning that will be felt and witnessed by others, particularly by those who come to our services seeking assistance; therefore, it is learning that is profoundly relevant.

This is the kind of formative professional development and leadership education that is respectful of otherness, that takes everyone seriously, that demonstrates our belief that the past is both significant and of no significance, and that we are all hard-wired to grow. It is this kind of formative professional development that suits the contemporary workplace which is characterised by pluralism and diversity,[63] that recognises that the present context is one where people of different faiths work side by side with people of no professed faith.

Towards Synthesis

Engaging people, exploring possibilities, and enabling passions is just one way that the contemporary leader might work with his or her people so that they can give of, and be, their best in nurturing change in the world. And looking for what will support the leader to empower and facilitate change in the organisation, to develop strategies for deep learning – where the head, the heart, and the spirit grow and expand – offers a framework for formative professional development and leadership education. Being conscious of continuity and discontinuity, of change and challenge, of strategy and everyday practice in their organisations, transformational leaders recognise that deep change is predicated on deep learning and that this only comes about by choice not by chance.

---

63 See Lieven Boeve, "Religion after Detraditionalisation: Christian Faith in a Post-Secular Europe", *Irish Theological Quarterly*, 70, 2005, pp. 99-122.

8
Position Vacant/Position Filled – Mission Flourishing! Getting Recruitment and Induction Right

David Beaver and Peter Hudson

Introduction

Centacare, Catholic Diocese of Ballarat Inc., commits itself to promoting and defending human rights, relying on the moralities of social justice, fairness, love and responsibility. In order to communicate these moralities to a diverse staff and to a secular public, it also re-articulates its Catholic identity by reflecting on the relationship between Catholic Social Teaching and the more widely known Universal Declaration of Human Rights.

Centacare Ballarat has, like many organisations, identified the employment of staff who are sympathetic to its mission and values as one of the most strategic tasks it has to accomplish if it is to be a high-performing organisation. This is a difficult task at the best of times but is made more difficult for Centacare because it operates in regional and rural Victoria and because the Catholic 'brand' has been damaged by many counts of clergy abuse throughout the Diocese of Ballarat.

To assist in this task, Centacare has engaged the services of Insync Surveys which specialises in the measurement and improvement of employee, customer, board and other stakeholder engagement. These services help and resource organisations on their journey towards sustained high performance.

This chapter shares some of the insights and outcomes of Centacare's journey of engaging in a professional partnership in the quest for greater commitment and high performance across the length and breadth of the organisation.

Context

The Catholic Diocese of Ballarat encompasses a vast area of northern and western Victoria with cities such as Ballarat, Mildura, Warrnambool, Horsham, Swan Hill and Hamilton within its jurisdiction.

The social services arm of the Diocese of Ballarat, known as Centacare, has approximately 200 staff offering a broad range of programs and services in mental health, homelessness and advocacy, family relationships, and family and youth support. The vast majority of these programs are government-funded and therefore have the usual compliance and assessment criteria dictating operations and expenditure.

Centacare was founded in 1977 in Mildura. While its mission and vision have developed over the intervening 36 years, they have remained centred on Catholic Social Teaching, as will be explained later in this chapter.

Centacare's guiding set of principles, which have been developed by staff over time, are as follows:

> **Our Vision** – Life-giving communities in a just society.
>
> **Our Mission** – To provide services which empower people to live with choice and opportunity.
>
> **Our Values**
> - *Respect* – We treat everyone with respect and dignity.
> - *Inclusion* – We build inclusive communities that value and embrace diversity.

- *Integrity* – We act according to our values in working for a fair and just society.
- *Accountability* – We act honestly and transparently and take responsibility for our actions.

A major challenge for an organisation such as Centacare is the perennial issue of staff turnover, both in the long and short term. How does Centacare continue to employ skilled specialist professionals with a clear appreciation of and energy for the mission of this Catholic agency?

Major factors to take into consideration are mission drift; the need for comprehensive and consistent recruitment processes; the relative isolation and size of many of the projects or offices of the organisation across regional Victoria; and the continuing diverse growth of the organisation as it responds to sector challenges and local needs.

So, why bother with trying to maintain a committed, skilled staff? Firstly, a committed, skilled staff means Centacare can provide a quality service to its clients, a service to which they have a right. Secondly, maintaining such a staff and minimising staff turnover will save money which can be re-invested into services. A study by Insync Surveys shows that a decrease of five per cent turnover will result in a saving of more than $200,000.[64] The Table 1 below demonstrates this saving.

Table 1: Savings in Relation to Reduced Staff Turnover

Number of staff	100
Turnover rate	18%
Indicative average salary	$60,000
Turnover costs	75%
Total cost of 18% turnover (100 x 0.18 x 60,000 x 0.75)	$810,000
Total cost of 13% turnover (aimed 5% reduction)	$585,000

---

64 Insync Surveys, *The 2012 Insync Surveys Retention Review*, 2012.

Why Do People Leave?

The most appropriate way of reducing turnover is to identify and respond to the causes of people leaving. Factors that cause people to leave can be classified as:

- the job (enrichment);
- structural issues;
- interpersonal issues;
- home life;
- environmental issues.

Surveys have shown that people report that turnover drivers in community services are job satisfaction (40%); balancing work and life demands (39%); work stress (38%); career opportunities (34%); and professional development (31%).

Single internal factors can be a lack of job enrichment (15%); structural reasons (pay, work stress, etc.) (10%); and interpersonal reasons (4%). On the other hand, multiple internal factors can be all of job enrichment, structural and interpersonal factors (14%); a combination of job enrichment and structural factors (14%); a combination of job enrichment and interpersonal factors (5%); or a combination of structural and interpersonal factors (3%).

What is an Organisation Able to Influence?

Organisational research indicates that 80 per cent of staff turnover is in the employer's control. Insync Surveys would propose that the following actions represent a proactive strategy from an organisation in response to the above-mentioned factors:

- measure, analyse and roadmap,
- create enriching and meaningful jobs,

- accommodate changing life circumstances,
- nurture an inclusive and positive workforce culture,
- enable and recognise performance.[65]

Survey

Insync Surveys' high performance framework which Centacare follows has been designed around two of the most important drivers of high performance, namely alignment and engagement. The surveys attempt to establish whether the day-to-day operations of the organisation are aligned with its strategic goals, and whether employees are engaged.[66]

The framework is based on research by David Weiss and Vince Molinaro[67] and rankings between 1 and 100 compared Centacare to other organisations in the benchmark database. The higher the ranking the better so that organisations with high engagement and low alignment are defined as 'passionate', whereas those with low engagement and high alignment are defined as 'driven'.

The research reveals that a high-performing organisation will:
- *Energise* employees to be inspired by the organisation and its senior leadership team. The organisation will have a clear and engaging long-term direction and purpose and the senior leadership will be good role models and motivate employees to achieve the organisation's goals.
- *Execute* the achievement of its long-term goals by aligning its plans and activities. Its line managers will set a good example and build effective collaborative teams with

---

65 Ibid.
66 Insync Surveys, *The 7 Organisational Habits that Drive High Performance*, 2013, p. 21.
67 David S. Weiss and Vince Molinaro, *The Leadership Gap: Building Leadership Capacity for Competitive Advantage*, John Wiley & Sons Canada Ltd, Ontario, 2005.

a strong accountability and performance culture. The organisation will invest in the development of its people and systems and be appropriately externally focussed on meeting its client and stakeholder needs.
- *Engage* employees who will be proud to work for their organisation. They will understand why their success is important for the organisation and they will recommend the organisation as a good place to work.

Within these framework areas are a total of 10 high performance factors which are important for the achievement of sustainable high performance. Each factor measures the extent to which employees perceive that the organisation is achieving best practice in the relevant area (see Figure 1 following page):[68]

Energise
- long-term direction,
- senior leadership;

Execute
- team leadership,
- team effectiveness,
- accountability culture,
- performance culture,
- investment in people,
- investment in systems,
- external focus;

Engage
- engagement.

---

68 Insync Surveys, *The 7 Organisational Habits that Drive High Performance,* 2013, p. 22.

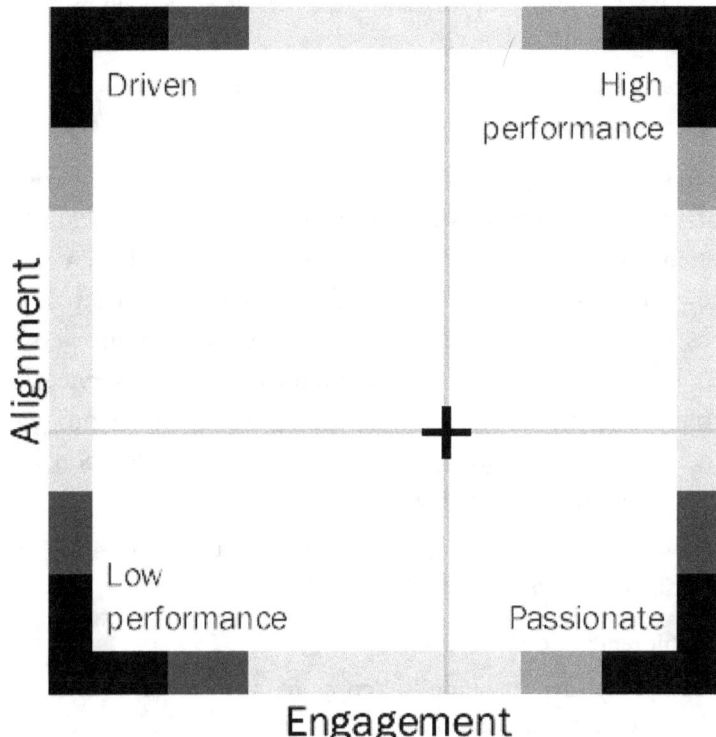

Figure 1: The Nature of Engagement

Findings

Centacare profiled as a 'passionate' organisation which manifested higher levels of engagement than alignment. A particular strength upon which to gain leverage is the strong emotional attachment of staff to the organisation and the work they do. Areas for improvement opportunity focussed around:

- clarifying the organisation's long-term direction and aims at all levels;

- supporting leaders to cascade these messages throughout Centacare; and
- investing in the leadership and management capabilities of program managers.

As a result of the above findings, Centacare has set in motion a series of workplace initiatives in such areas as the development of a comprehensive Centacare Workforce Plan and the implementation of a new Human Resource Information System. In recent times there has also been the appointment of an Agency Identity person who has been developing material for induction and in-service for all personnel within the organisation. There is a progressive program in place for creating 'Leading Teams' across the organisation and developing more flexible employment practices.

In Centacare's efforts to recruit the 'right people' for our organisation we are doing the following:

- comprehensive advertisements,
- comprehensive position descriptions that require key selection criteria to be completed at time of application,
- panel interviews with generally three key people including program/general manager, coordinator and human resources representative,
- second-round interviews if we need to delve further or discern between two close candidates,
- online behaviour profiling such as DISC (dominance, inducement, submission, compliance)[69] if we feel we need to know more about a candidate,
- comprehensive reference checking,
- working with children checks and police checks,

---

69 For information on DISC, see talenttools.com.au/ – accessed on 15 January 2014.

- induction and orientation program (including new 'buddy' system),
- six-month probation period,
- monthly formal supervision with line manager.

Of course, all the best recruitment processes in the world are found wanting if the organisation is not able to engage and hold these quality people for a significant period of professional and personal growth. Holding the right people leads the organisation to explore creatively many of the following options:

- continuing formation in the ethos of the agency and its values, purpose and mission,
- Centacare as a supportive workplace with a caring nature,
- family-friendly workplace including flexibility if required,
- paid maternity leave,
- salary sacrificing arrangements,
- purchase of leave,
- generous personal leave entitlements,
- professional development,
- training (e-learning resources),[70]
- performance reviews,
- employee assistance program.

Catholic Social Teaching and Human Rights[71]

As stated in the introduction, underlying all this organisational scrutiny and development is the creative tension that sits with the organisation

---
70 For sources of e-learning resources, see ccinsurance.org.au and harvardbusiness.org/harvard-managementor – accessed on 15 January 2014.
71 Dr Richard Wade, pamphlet (Draft 5), Centacare internal discussion paper, Australian Catholic University, 2013.

expressing its identity as both a demonstrably Catholic agency and as a first-rate human services provider. Is there a distinction? Does there need to be one? What is intrinsic to the Ballarat Catholic Church's provision of social services in the spirit of the Gospel which makes them remarkable (not better) amongst providers? These questions are important as increasingly staff do not identify themselves as Catholic. Also, as stated previously, clergy sexual abuse throughout the Diocese of Ballarat has cast a shadow over Catholic agencies and their personnel. This has resulted in the need for Centacare to re-articulate its Catholic identity by reflecting on the relationship between Catholic Social Teaching and the more universally appreciated Universal Declaration of Human Rights.

If, in this context, we hope to maintain our justice values of respect, inclusion, integrity and accountability, we must be clear about how we apply these in our work lives. What they mean to us and to those we serve must be explicit. They must express the overall aim and purpose of Centacare, without ambiguity. All stakeholders of Centacare should have no doubt that we are grounded in the principles of justice, and therefore that we are agents of change. We stand against the trend and are prepared to align ourselves with those who support the same principles.

As an institution we are supported by a well-developed set of principles which speak clearly to the moralities of social justice, fairness, love and responsibility. These are commonly referred to as Catholic Social Teaching, which emphasises dignity, solidarity, subsidiarity and the common good. The substance of Catholic Social Teaching can be readily applied in diverse situations as we work with our clients, regardless of personal religious affiliation.

Centacare is a Catholic social service agency committed to promoting and defending human rights. Human rights are a central expression of Centacare's service and the Christian vision of life in society. Centacare's ministry of human rights is tightly linked to its religious identity which upholds the conviction that rights are grounded in the dignity and nature of the human person created in the image of God.

Rights language is another way of expressing our common morality and common humanity. The hope is that we can see that we are essentially like others in morally relevant ways, and others are similar to us. The ministry of Centacare's human rights ethic is a mutual task shared by all staff. Rights are moral standards that hold everyone accountable and empower individuals to claim and demand what is due to them. As such, rights are a meaningful and recognised commitment to the protection of the dignity of staff and clients against injustice, oppression, invasion of privacy, and intolerance. Centacare acknowledges that rights are expressions of an individual's freedom to claim particular benefits/goods (e.g., the right to freedom of conscience and religion) or forbearance of harm to self and property (e.g., the right not to be unfairly dismissed, right to life, and justice in business matters). Rights serve to signpost and protect the authority of the individual, in relation to society as a whole and in relation to other individuals.

Human rights, although they are expressed as rights of the individual, are understood by Centacare also to have a fundamental connection to the common good. The common good is "the sum total of social conditions which allow people, either as groups or as individuals, to reach their fulfilment more fully and more easily".[72] This understanding of human rights is interconnected with Centacare's belief about the truth of the human person, which is that the nature of the human person is both social and individual. The common good (human flourishing, dignity, rights, duties, justice, participation

---

72 *Catechism of the Catholic Church*, number 1906, Libreria Editrice Vaticana, Citta del Vaticano, 1993.

and common goals) which binds together individuals and societies in equality is served by protecting individual rights within the ethical framework of duties.

In the light of this, Centacare is further articulating its duties and responsibilities by developing a possible checklist of expected behaviours which could be used for a range of recruitment and performance measures. The list contains the following to this point:

- acknowledge and respect the rights of others;
- have a preferential duty/responsibility to provide justice for the underprivileged and the vulnerable;
- act with prudence on behalf of clients;
- collaborate mutually;
- respect individual autonomy;
- care for clients with sensitivity;
- act for others in a responsible manner;
- respect the confidentiality and privacy of clients;
- preserve life and live life with integrity;
- listen and speak to clients respectfully;
- respect the freedom of religion, thought and conscience.

By continuing our engagement with staff in this discussion around Catholic Social Teaching and human rights and by continuing to implement improved human resource practices as outlined above, Centacare hopes to build a more highly skilled workforce committed to its vision and mission as a Catholic organisation. Most importantly, this commitment will lead to increased and better outcomes for those on the margins of our society with whom we are called to walk.

9

The Changing Face of the Catholic Community in Australia: Challenges for Catholic Social Service Organisations

Robert Dixon

Since it was founded in 1996, the Pastoral Research Office of the Australian Catholic Bishops Conference has carried out numerous studies of the Catholic community in Australia, covering topics such as the demographics of the Catholic population, the practices, beliefs and attitudes of Mass attenders, the reasons why people do and do not go to Mass, and changes in the numerical strength of Australia's Catholic religious congregations. The staff of the office can therefore speak with some authority about the changing face of our Catholic community, and we can identify and raise many of the challenges that face Church agencies and organisations, including Catholic social service agencies. In this way, we can assist agencies and organisations to remain true to their mission.

In this chapter, I cover, in a quick overview, the contemporary situation with regard to:

- The Catholic Population in Australia.
- Mass-attending Catholics.
- The Impact of Cultural Change on Mass Attenders.
- The Importance of Attendance *and* Identification for Christian Belief.

As I do this, I am going to call occasionally on the assistance of that highly esteemed Columban priest and anthropologist, Fr Cyril Hally, who died in 2010 at the age of 90. Fr Hally's contribution will be in the form of extracts from a chapter he wrote for a 1982 book on Christianity in Australia.[73]

The Catholic Population in Australia

When I speak of the Catholic population, I am referring to all those who ticked the "Catholic" box (or who had it ticked for them) at Question 19 in the Australian Census on 9 August 2011. The Catholic population also includes those who, rather than ticking the box, wrote in "Catholic", or some variety of Catholic, in the space provided. People belonging to the Eastern Catholic Churches, such as the Maronite, Melkite, Chaldean and Ukrainian Catholic Churches, were encouraged to do just that, so that we could get an indication of their numbers.

According to the 2011 Australian Census, there were 5,439,268 Catholics in a total Australian population of 21,507,719.[74] This means that Catholics make up just over a quarter (25.3 per cent) of the Australian population, making them Australia's largest religious group.

One of the most striking features of the Catholic population is its ethnic diversity. Catholics are more likely to come from a non-English speaking country than Australians who are not Catholic: 17.9 per cent of Catholics were born in a non-English speaking country, compared to 14.9 per cent of people who are not Catholic. Overall, nearly a

---

73 Cyril Hally, "Growth patterns in the Catholic Church" in *The Shape of Belief*, edited by D. Harris et al., Lancer Press, Homebush, 1982.
74 For a full profile of the Catholic population in the 2011 Census, see Robert Dixon and Stephen Reid, "The contemporary Catholic community: A view from the 2011 Census", *Australasian Catholic Record*, 2013, 90(2), pp. 131-146.

quarter of Australia's Catholics (23.6 per cent) were born overseas. In addition, there were 124,618 Catholics of Aboriginal and Torres Strait Islander origin – 2.3 per cent of all Australia's Catholics, and 22.7 per cent of all Indigenous Australians.

The main countries in which Australia's Catholics were born are shown in Table 1. The largest group of Catholic immigrants are the Italians. Most Italian Catholics arrived in Australia in the 1950s and 1960s, so that now almost two-thirds of them are aged 60 or more. In contrast, almost 90 per cent of Catholics born in the Philippines are aged under 60, so that it is highly probable that by the time of the next census in 2016, the Philippines will have displaced Italy as the overseas country contributing the highest number of Catholics to the Australian population. Catholics born in the Sudan or South Sudan (there were 7,983 of them in 2011) have the youngest age profile, with almost 80 per cent being under the age of 40.

Associated with the ethnic diversity of the Catholic community is the fact that Australia's Catholics speak a wide range of languages other than English at home, the most common (in diminishing order) being Italian, Filipino languages, Spanish, Arabic, Vietnamese, Croatian, Chinese languages, Polish and Maltese. Italian was spoken at home by almost 267,000 Catholics, an indication of the strength of Italian family and cultural identity, since the number of Catholics born in Italy, just under 169,000, was almost 100,000 smaller than the number of Catholics speaking Italian at home. Eighty per cent of Australia's Catholics speak only English at home.

In 1982, Fr Hally noted that "as immigrants from overseas Catholic communities enter the Australian Church they bring with them a rich variety of symbols, understandings and practices". This has certainly been shown to be true, perhaps to an even greater extent than he anticipated, as we shall see below.

Table 1. Major Birthplaces of Australian Catholics, 2011

Countries	Catholics
Australia	4,065,104
Italy	168,801
United Kingdom (except Northern Ireland)	137,209
Philippines	134,655
New Zealand	73,145
Ireland (including Northern Ireland)	56,309
Croatia and other parts of former Yugoslavia	49,197
India	48,209
Vietnam	39,892
Malta	37,816
Poland	36,117
Germany	30,478
Lebanon	28,004
Netherlands	24,861
China (including Hong Kong)	22,423
Sri Lanka	20,216
South Africa	19,978
Iraq	17,184
Indonesia	16,821
Malaysia	16,791
South Korea	16,705
Mauritius	16,072
Regions	**Catholics**
Central and South America	67,471
Other European countries	62,050
Middle East and North Africa	26,572
Other South East Asian countries	22,978
North America	22,743

Source: Australian Bureau of Statistics – 2011 Census of Population and Housing. Countries and regions where more than 16,000 Australian Catholics were born.

In the same chapter, Fr Hally predicted that "given the tendency to interfaith marriage and the fact that nearly half Catholic children do not attend Catholic schools, we can predict a substantial decline in the number of Catholics in the immediate future".[75] Both the conditions were true then and continue to be true, but there has been no decline in the number of Catholics. For example, in the five years between the 2006 and 2011 Censuses, the number of Catholics increased by more than 312,000, or 6.1 per cent. Catholics have continued to grow in numbers at every census, although their percentage of the Australian population has been declining slowly since the peak of 27.3 per cent in 1991, meaning that they are growing at a slower rate than the non-Catholic population.

This continuing growth cannot be attributed to immigration: the percentage of the Catholic population born in Australia has remained virtually constant at around 75 per cent since at least 1991. Growth might have been higher were it not for the phenomenon of *disidentification*. If there was ever a time when it was true that "Once a Catholic, always a Catholic", it is certainly not true now. It is estimated that, across all age groups, more than 20,000 Australians cease to identify as Catholics every year, with more than half of these aged between 20 and 29.[76] This phenomenon has important consequences for the level of Christian belief in Australia, as we shall see a little later.

If disidentification has some important consequences, so too does identification as a Catholic. In one sense, identification on the census form defines the limits of the Catholic community in Australia. Within that population of more than 5.4 million, there is a broad

---

75 Hally, Cyril, op. cit., p. 87. In 2011, 68.7 per cent of couples in a registered marriage involving at least one Catholic were couples of mixed religion, and 52.8 per cent of Catholic children attended Catholic schools.
76 Dixon, Robert and Reid, Stephen, op cit., p. 145.

spectrum of involvement and belief, from very active participants in the life of their parish, school or other Catholic organisation to those for whom their Catholic identity means little else than the tick on the census form. But even in those cases there is some evidence that identification makes a difference.

The detailed census data acquired by the Pastoral Research Office and available free of charge to every Catholic agency and organisation in Australia[77] therefore paints a comprehensive demographic picture of the community that underlies and provides bedrock support for Catholic social services of all types. It can also inform agencies about the nature of the Catholic community in an area, right down to local parish level, and suggest the type of needs that may exist in that area. For example, the available census data can provide information on family structure and family income, on couple families where both partners are Catholic and where only one partner is Catholic, on one-parent families, on couples in registered marriages and couples in *de facto* relationships, on elderly Catholics and school-aged children, on Catholics living alone, on Catholics who are unemployed, on recently arrived immigrants and on immigrants who cannot speak English well, on people who need assistance with core activities such as eating and showering and on those who provide assistance to such people, and on people who do voluntary work in the community. Is there a Catholic social services agency anywhere in Australia that is not interested in one or more of those groups?

Mass-attending Catholics

Fr Hally's prediction of a "substantial decline" in the Catholic population "in the immediate future" did not come to pass. But while

---

[77] For further information, contact the Pastoral Research Office; see pro.catholic.org.au – accessed on 17 January 2014.

Catholics in the main have retained their Catholic identity, they have become much less likely to attend Sunday Mass, leading to large falls in attendances. In 2011, the number of people at Mass in Australia on a typical weekend was about 662,000, or 12.2 per cent of the total number of Catholics.[78] In 1982, Fr Hally was concerned that "in many parishes attendance at weekly Sunday Mass may be no higher than 35 per cent",[79] when less than 30 years earlier the attendance rate across Australia had been in the vicinity of 70 per cent.

Attendances have been in a more or less constant state of decline since the 1950s,[80] but until 1996 there was little information available about who went to Mass and how the profile of attenders was changing over time. Between 1996 and 2011, the percentage of Mass attenders born in non-English speaking countries rose from just over 18 per cent to over 33 per cent, resulting in an increase of attenders born in non-English speaking countries of about 69,000. But, during the same period, despite the increase in the number of attenders from non-English speaking countries, overall Mass attendances declined by about 23 per cent. This happened because the number of Australian-born attenders fell by around one-third! Two major factors have

---

78 There are two main sources of data about Mass attendance. The Australian Catholic Bishops Conference Pastoral Research Office's National Counts of Attendance (2001, 2006 and 2011) collected attendance figures from all parishes and other Mass centres, as well as information about each Mass, such as the language of celebration. The National Church Life Surveys (2001, 2006 and 2011), and the 1996 Catholic Church Life Survey, were conducted in a national random sample of parishes, and provide a great deal of information about Mass attenders, including their frequency of attendance, their demographic characteristics and their beliefs and practices. In 2011, a total of 47,426 completed questionnaires were received from the 217 parishes in the national sample.
79 Hally, Cyril, op. cit., p. 86.
80 See Robert Dixon and Ruth Powell, "Vatican II: A data-based analysis of its impact on Australian Catholic life", in Neil Ormerod et al. (eds), *Vatican II: Reception and Implementation in the Australian Church*, Garratt Publishing, Mulgrave, 2012, p. 302.

contributed to this decline. Firstly, people in particular age cohorts have stopped going to Mass; it is estimated, for example, that up to 26,000 Baby Boomers stopped going to Mass between 1996 and 2011. Secondly, young adult attenders are not being replaced as they age. In 1996, about 136,000 Catholics aged 15 to 34 attended Mass on a typical weekend, but by 2011 the number of Mass attenders aged 15 to 34 had dropped to about 80,000.

The 2011 National Church Life Survey (NCLS) shows that about 85 per cent of those who attend in any one week are there every weekend, but the individuals who make up the other 15 per cent vary from week to week. Some are there two or three times a month, others only once a month, others less frequently still. NCLS results also show that 97.4 per cent of the people at Mass in parishes on weekends are Catholics, and that a further 2.2 per cent belong to other Christian denominations. In 2011, about one-third of all attenders aged 15 and over were aged between 60 and 74. Attenders aged 15 to 19 accounted for only four per cent while people aged 80 or more made up more than eight per cent of attenders.

In general, Mass attenders are older, better educated and more likely to be female and to have been born overseas than the Catholic population as a whole. About three-fifths of Mass attenders are female, and about one-third have a university degree, compared to 18 per cent of all Catholics aged 15 and over. While 75 per cent of the Catholic population were born in Australia, less than 60 per cent of Mass attenders were. One-third were born in non-English speaking countries. In particular, respondents born in India, Sri Lanka or the Philippines accounted for much larger proportions of attenders compared to their proportions in the Catholic population as a whole. Catholics from these countries not only have better attendance rates than Australian-born Catholics but they are younger as well.

As Figure 1 illustrates, attendance rates vary considerably by age. Among young Catholic adults aged 20-34, only about five or six per cent attend Mass on a typical Sunday. The highest attendance rates are found among those in their 70s, where attendance is typically a little over 30 per cent.

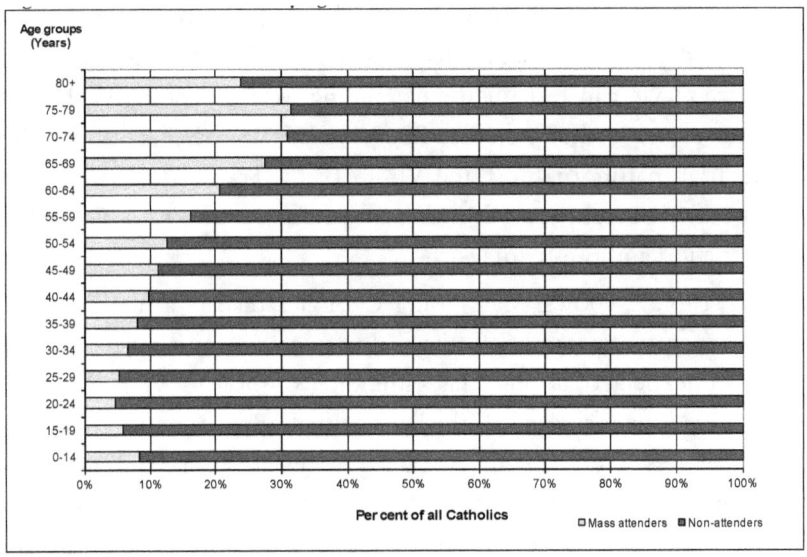

Derived from 2011 National Count of Attendance, 2011 Australian Census of Population and Housing, and 2011 National Church Life Survey.

Figure 1. Mass Attendance Rates by Age, 2011

The Church in Australia owes much to our immigrants, particularly those from non-English speaking countries. But at the same time, we are experiencing a major decline in attendance among Australian-born Catholics. Back in 1982, Fr Hally noted that "unlike the schooling crisis, which is being recognised and tackled, the parish crisis remains concealed from most Catholics".[81] I wonder what he would say today?

---

81 Hally, Cyril, op. cit., p. 83.

Impact of Cultural Change on Mass Attenders[82]

In 1982, Fr Hally observed that "economic, political, social, religious and cultural changes in the rest of society cannot fail to affect the Catholic quarter of the population".[83] Have these changes affected the beliefs of even the most active Catholics, and are the effects more pronounced among those who were born in Australia (and other Western countries) compared to those who were born in non-Western countries? We can test this by examining Mass-attending Catholics' responses to six items in the 2011 NCLS: their beliefs about the Trinitarian nature of God, the Virgin Birth, Transubstantiation and the bodily Resurrection of Christ, and their attitudes to the morality of abortion and pre-marital sex.

As Table 2 shows, Mass-going Catholics display a high level of acceptance of the four key Catholic doctrines. This level of orthodoxy is not unexpected among Mass-attending Catholics. What might be considered surprising is that the level of orthodoxy is not even higher. Nevertheless, there is some variation: older attenders and attenders born in non-Western countries, particularly India, Sri Lanka and the Philippines, tend to hold more orthodox views than attenders who are younger or born in Australia.

When we look at the two central moral teachings, we find that most Mass attenders are strongly opposed to abortion, although only 51 per cent in the 2011 NCLS said that abortion is always morally wrong. The total opposed to abortion rises to 86 per cent when one takes into account the 35 per cent who said that abortion can be

---

[82] For a full discussion of these questions, see Robert Dixon, "What Do Mass Attenders Believe? Contemporary Cultural Change and the Acceptance of Key Catholic Beliefs and Moral Teachings by Australian Mass Attenders", *Australasian Catholic Record*, 2013, 90(4), pp. 439-458.

[83] Hally, Cyril, op. cit., p. 78.

Table 2. Mass Attenders' Views of Key Catholic Moral Teachings and Beliefs, 2011

	Mass Attenders (%)
Abortion	
Always morally wrong	51
Justified only in extreme circumstances	35
Justified widely but not always	13
Never wrong	1
Number of responses = 1,511	
Premarital sex	
Always morally wrong	42
Not wrong if in a committed relationship	51
Never wrong	8
Number of responses = 1,540	
Understanding of God	
There is one God, three divine persons: Father, Son and Holy Spirit	84
God exists, and is a divine person, but not Father, Son and Holy Spirit	3
God is the name we give to a higher power in the universe, the mysterious and creative source of life	7
We and the universe are in God, part of God, identified with God	3
God is not 'out there', but is found only within each person	2
We cannot know for sure if God exists	1
God does not exist	0
Number of responses = 2,470	

Virginity of Mary	
Mary gave birth to Jesus without having had sexual intercourse	75
Mary's virginity is not meant to be taken literally	25
Number of responses = 2,398	
Eucharist: the Consecrated Bread and Wine ...	
... truly become the sacred Body and Blood of Christ	90
... remain bread and wine	10
Number of responses = 2,410	
Resurrection	
Christ was raised by God's power from death to life – really, bodily, physically	71
Christ rose from the dead, not literally, but in the Christian community's faith in God's power to give life	24
Christ did not rise in any sense	0
Don't know	4
Number of responses = 2,464	

Source: National Church Life Survey 2011, Questionnaire versions S3 and X.

Note: data have been weighted to take account of different levels of diocesan participation. Catholic respondents only; also, due to rounding error, percentages may not add to 100 per cent.

justified in extreme circumstances, such as rape and because of risk to the mother's life, but the Church teaches that neither these nor any other factors constitute grounds for abortion. It is clear that only a small proportion of respondents (13 per cent) are prepared to consider that abortion can be widely justified, and almost none (1 per cent) believe that abortion is never wrong. On the other hand, when it comes to pre-marital sex, there is a stark contrast between the

Church's teaching (pre-marital sex is always morally wrong) and the views of Mass attenders, with only 42 per cent accepting the Church's teaching. About half (51 per cent) say that it is not wrong if the man and the woman "are committed to a long-term relationship", and eight per cent say that pre-marital sex is "not wrong in any circumstances". Unsurprisingly, attenders aged 15-34 are the least likely to say that pre-marital sex is always wrong (33 per cent), but what is perhaps surprising is that only half (50 per cent) of attenders aged 60 or more hold that view. For both issues, being born in non-Western countries strongly increased the likelihood of being in agreement with the Church's teaching. Not only do people from non-Western countries make up an ever-increasing proportion of Mass attenders, they are also far more likely than Australian-born attenders to hold orthodox beliefs.

What is the cause of this difference between attenders born in Western countries compared to those born in non-Western countries? It appears that Fr Hally was right: changes in society do affect how Catholics think. Australian scholars Gary Bouma[84] and Gerald Rose,[85] drawing on Max Weber,[86] argue that the key shift driving the changes in the culture is the shift from rational and traditional authority to experiential authority. In their view, this "experiential shift" is foundational to all other changes in Western culture in the last 50 years, leading to a situation where ultimate authority "is to be found in the individual's experiences, senses and feelings".[87] Experience has

---

[84] Gary Bouma, *Australian Soul: Religion and Spirituality in the 21st Century*, Cambridge University Press, Melbourne, 2006.

[85] Gerald Rose, *Re-imagining Church: Producing Sacred Spaces for the Experience of the Transcendent in an Evolving Experiential Culture*, PhD thesis, Monash University, 2013.

[86] Max Weber, *Max Weber on Charisma and Institution Building: Selected Papers*, edited and with an Introduction by S. N. Eisenstadt, University of Chicago Press, Chicago, 1968.

[87] Bouma, Gary, op. cit., p. 90.

replaced reason and tradition as the basis of authority. The result is that traditional forms of authority are no longer held in the respect that they were previously, and many older patterns of ministry practice are no longer effective.[88] The impact of the experiential shift on the culture in lessening acceptance of Catholic beliefs and moral attitudes has been principally confined to Australian-born attenders and those born in other English speaking countries and Europe. To be effective in communicating to people born in Australia and other Western countries these days, Church teachings must resonate with their experience.[89]

These results have many pastoral implications, not least for catechesis and adult faith education in parishes, and for the leadership by and training of priests. Nearly five million Australian Catholics were born either in Australia or in other Western countries, and in the majority of cases their worldview has been largely shaped by the experiential nature of contemporary culture. Unless we take that experiential shift seriously, our efforts in evangelisation, catechesis and pastoral care are likely to lack effectiveness.

The Importance of Attendance *and* Identification for Christian Belief

I mentioned earlier that Catholic identification has important consequences for belief. There is also a strong connection between church-going and belief. One illustration of both these points comes from the Australian data in the 2009 Australian Survey of Social Attitudes. A random sample of Australians were asked whether or not they agreed that "Jesus' Resurrection from the dead was an actual

---

88 Rose, Gerald, op. cit., p. 92.
89 See Dixon, Robert, "What do Mass Attenders Believe", op. cit., p. 457.

historical event". The results for different religious groups are shown in Table 3. Although we might quibble about the meaning of the phrase "historical event", most people would probably agree that the question provides a measure of the level of acceptance of a central Christian belief. There are some surprises; firstly, the size of the gap between Catholic and Protestant Christians (60 per cent of the former compared to 49 per cent of the latter expressed agreement with the statement) and, secondly, that a relatively high percentage of people from non-Christian religions (44 per cent) agree with the statement, although the small number of respondents (33) in that category may be a factor there.

Table 3 Percentage of Respondents Expressing Agreement with the Statement "Jesus' Resurrection from the Dead was an Actual Historical Event"

	Agree or strongly agree (%)
Religious Groups	
Catholics	60
Other Christians	49
People belonging to non-Christian religions	44
People of no religion	5
Effect of Attendance and Identification	
Mass-attending Catholics	83
Non-attending Catholics	49
Raised Catholic but now no religion	4

Source: Australian Survey of Social Attitudes 2009.
Number of Respondents (unweighted) = 975, including 335 Catholics.

Now let us look at the effect of attendance and also of *identification*. I sometimes hear it said that people who just tick the Catholic box in the census and have no other engagement with the Church are not 'real' Catholics, and that the Christian faith does not make any difference to them. But identification *does* make a difference: people who continue to identify as Catholics are far more likely than people who were raised as Catholics – but who now have no religion – to agree or strongly agree that Jesus' Resurrection was an actual historical event (49 per cent compared to 4 per cent). In fact, those who were once Catholic but who now have no religion are no more likely than other people of no religion to agree that Jesus' Resurrection was an actual historical event. Here we see pretty convincing evidence that attendance at church is powerfully related to belief, but that even the mere fact of identification as a Catholic also makes a big difference.

Conclusion

In this chapter I have highlighted a number of the challenges facing the Catholic Church in Australia, challenges which have repercussions for the social service agencies which are an essential arm of the Church's mission. They include, among others, the challenge of the changing face of the Catholic community, the diversity of needs that exist within that community, declining attendances at Mass, particularly among men, young adults and the Australian-born, the changing attitude to traditional forms of authority and the increasing reliance on personal experience as the foundation for belief and moral decision-making. These challenges are real and urgent, and it is impossible for Catholic social service agencies to remain true to their mission without coming to an understanding of the changing face of the Catholic community. In 1982, Fr Hally wrote that "the times call for the development of a new identity and *modus vivendi* by the Catholic Church as an institution, in continuity with the past and open to the future".⁹⁰ The call is even more urgent now, and the need for a new *modus vivendi* has been recognised by no less than Pope Francis who, as Archbishop of Buenos Aires, wrote that:

> The defining aspect of this change of epoch is that things are no longer in their place. Our previous ways of explaining the world and relationships, good and bad, no longer appear to work. The way in which we locate ourselves in history has changed. Things we thought would never happen, or that we never thought we would see, we are experiencing now, and we dare not even imagine the future. That which appeared normal to us – family, the Church, society and the world – will probably no longer seem that way. We cannot simply wait for what we are experiencing to pass, under the illusion that things will return to being how they were before.⁹¹

---

90 Hally, Cyril, op. cit., p. 87.
91 Cardinal Jorge Bergoglio (Pope Francis), Aparecida document presented during the Fifth Conference of Latin American Bishops, 2007, quoted in "Priests to face epoch change as a challenge to seek out the remote"; accessed on 28 January 2014 at visnews-en.blogspot.com.au.

PART THREE

Personal Reflections

10

Greatly Amused: Mary MacKillop and the One Habit of a Highly Effective Leader

Michael McGirr

We have a magnet on our fridge at home which carries the words of Mary MacKillop: "I had time to be greatly amused." I suspect that if Mary MacKillop knew that her words were going to end up on fridge magnets she might not have said them in the first place, but that is beside the point. The magnet does not say where this quote comes from, which is a bonus because I like to think it is the kind of thing Mary MacKillop would have said often. She had a light-hearted spirit, even in the heaviest of circumstances.

This is part of her enduring gift to us. The fridge magnet says that she had time, which is another reason to admire her, especially because fridge doors tend to be littered with reminders of how little time we think we have. When lives get crowded and overloaded to breaking point, humour is among the first casualties and is often replaced by cynicism, the frozen and brittle version of humour. Mary MacKillop was not like that. She knew that God saw the funny side and this is central to her vision of leadership. It was warm and spacious.

Mary MacKillop was beatified in January 1995 on a very hot day at Randwick Racecourse. Pope John Paul II came to Australia to lead the celebration and there were many other dignitaries as well. A week before the beatification, I was visiting a town called Trangie in western NSW, a small place on a long straight road between Dubbo and Bourke. My father died when I was in Year 12. As a young man, he had once owned a pub in Trangie and I had reached a time in my life when I wanted to visit his world. In Trangie, I happened to meet the local priest and he invited me to lunch. His name was Fr Peter Coyte.

To understand Peter, you needed to visit his presbytery which was modest to say the least. The back wall had fallen off in one entire piece and was lying in the yard with grass growing through it. This meant that the toilet was well aired but not especially private but this hardly mattered as the only onlookers were a few bored livestock. Beside the wall was a car park full of rusted wrecks as Peter drove his cars until they were exhausted and then simply allowed them to retire in his backyard. In the front yard was a merry-go-round which he had bought from a circus which went broke on its way through the town. The merry-go-round was also broken.

Inside, the walls were covered with Peter's artwork and his writing. He was no slouch as an artist. His sermons were all written out on the walls too. The place had three bedrooms, one for each year in the Sunday lectionary. Peter's sermons had been written on the walls of the relevant room so he knew where to find them when he needed them next time. Peter had been in Trangie for a long time and believed that the secret of clerical stability was letting the presbytery reach the point where nobody else would want it. I could not imagine he would ever face much competition for his job but I was touched that it meant so much to him.

When lunchtime arrived, Peter began to heat up an electric fry pan which stood on his kitchen bench. It was apparent that pan was seldom cleaned and the fat in it had congealed and did not smell too good. As it began to heat, Peter produced two antique pieces of meat from the fridge and brushed them with his handkerchief. He laid these on the fat and eased them down towards the element until they left a footprint. He then peeled two extremely ripe bananas, which were located beneath a pile of newspapers by using the sense of smell, and laid one in each footprint, pushing them down towards the meat with a fork. Finally, he spooned a little of the fat on to each portion. This was served with warm guava juice which had been donated by Indonesian tourists who also broke down in the town. The company was great but the meal itself was less than appetising.

That afternoon, I accompanied Peter to a funeral in the local cemetery where an Indigenous veteran of World War II was being buried. Peter did a wonderful job in helping to create a bridge between two communities, the Indigenous and the RSL, who do not always get along as well as they might. Shortly afterwards I headed off to Sydney for the beatification.

A month or so later, I received a letter from Fr Peter Coyte, enclosing a clipping from the Dubbo paper. There was a small article reporting the fact that the Trangie priest had recently received a most unexpected visit from several dignitaries, namely Cardinal Winning of Glasgow and then Archbishop O'Brien of Edinburgh. They had been visiting Australia from Scotland, where Mary MacKillop had family roots, for the beatification and Bishop Bill Brennan was showing them a little of the outback. My eye was arrested by one line in the report: "They stayed for lunch." Peter added underneath in biro "and they received the same cuisine, prepared by the same chef in the same manner as you yourself received".

Mary MacKillop is one of those terrific figures in the history of the Church who gets everyone to eat at the same table. Jesus, of course, was the expert at this. Her spirituality owes a great deal to small far-flung communities, places which have the uncanny capacity to create the gift of acceptance. Mary MacKillop ate what was on her plate, in every sense of the word. Her leadership started with acceptance. Her biography of Julian Tenison Woods is one of the most accepting books you could hope to read.

Like all of us, Mary's spiritual life was shaped by the unspiritual. She was the child of displaced parents and a confused father, a man who was at home neither in the world of the spirit (he left the seminary) nor the world of money (he was benighted in business). She was a child of grief who held her baby brother, Alick, as he died. She was about five when this happened. She was a child of no fixed address who lived in countless places in her life. She was a child of work; by the age of 14 she was helping to support her brothers and sisters. Somehow or other she got to be a saint. She got to be a saint by being herself. There is no other way nor is there any other way of becoming a leader as opposed to a controller.

Nevertheless, the one habit of Mary MacKillop on which I would like to dwell is her capacity to deal realistically with anxiety. It is well worth reading the letters between Mary and her mother, Flora, which have been most helpfully compiled in *Mary MacKillop and Flora* by Sheila McCreanor.[92]

The relationship between mothers and daughters is a tricky business, even for saints. I love one long letter which Mary wrote to her mother from Rome in June 1873. This was, as we all know, an anxious trip for Mary as she had been excommunicated by a man about whom the best one can say is that he was as much torment to himself as he was to others. The pope had welcomed Mary affably

---

92 Sheila McCreanor (ed.), *Mary MacKillop & Flora: Correspondence between Mary MacKillop and her Mother, Flora McDonald MacKillop*, Sisters of St Joseph of the Sacred Heart, North Sydney, 2004.

and the visit had gone well and her rule looked as if it would be accepted.

What I relish is the last page of this letter in which Mary says that she hopes to get "something nice" for her sister, Annie, and to which she adds a postscript (for which she needed to re-open the envelope) apologising for having forgotten to mention her mother's birthday. Mary also says: "I am getting quite fat." So, here is a young woman fighting for a vision that will have an enormous impact on the life of faith in Australia and, indeed, on our entire culture. But she is also a 31-year-old daughter concerned about relationships with siblings, with her mother and with her own body. You can almost see her getting around with a Lonely Planet Guide, except Mary never believed that the planet was lonely.

Mary's letters to her mother show a deep awareness of the price that anxiety forces the soul to pay. When she wrote in 1867 to tell her mother that she was henceforth to be known as Mary of the Cross, she said: "remember that all my anxieties and fears for your welfare have long since been laid at the foot of our Lord." Throughout 1866, as Mary embarked upon life in the habit, her letters to her mother are full of phrases such as "you must have moments, nay hours, of deep anxiety" and "don't dread the future" and "do not give way to dullness nor imagine evils which I hope will never come to pass" and "the thought of leaving you, my loved mother, gave me so much pain and anxiety" and "do not fear about the debts". There is a very obvious theme here and that theme is anxiety.

Anxiety is the plague of our culture and I believe leadership in a wide range of contexts means dealing with it and not being pushed around by it. We live in a society which is bullied by fear. In our political world, it is not hard to see how the anxiety button is used to trigger responses to everything from boat people to interest rates.

Many of the organisations for which we work are tied up in red tape and compliance issues that are often enough the fruit of anxiety. I teach teenagers whose world wants to make them anxious. I meet parents who are made to feel that their best efforts are somehow never quite adequate.

The thing that you do not hear often enough about teaching is that it is such good fun. I love the humour of young people and I believe that the path beyond fear to faith is held together by laughter. I often quote the line of Chesterton from the end of his wonderful book, *Orthodoxy*. Chesterton believed, with good reason, that Christianity was essentially comic because humans are ridiculous. He wrote: "we sit in the starry chamber of silence, while the laughter of the heavens is too loud for us to hear. Joy ... is the gigantic secret of the Christian."

One of the forms of anxiety which frustrates me the most is status anxiety, the need for many people in Catholic and other agencies to climb the tree and get ahead. In education, this is closely linked to credentialism, the appalling connection that is being made between the gaining of higher degrees and educational leadership. Just this year, I have become aware of two excellent people who have applied for positions as deputy principals in Catholic high schools. Both of them have thirty years experience of generous service to young people. They know and understand kids and have worked themselves into the ground of their behalf. Both received back replies to their applications saying that while they were fine candidates, they lacked the necessary higher degrees. This is total humbug. It means that people who are prepared to invest in themselves are preferred to those prepared to invest in others.

Do not get me wrong. I have a deep love of education and profoundly admire the commitment to postgraduate research of those who truly want to explore the life of the mind. But this is not what I see happening. I see people doing Master's courses, in which they learn very little as far as I can see, simply in order to improve their status. This is just plain wrong. Mary MacKillop might well have kicked her poor dog if she thought that credentialism would be the path to leadership in the educational world she did so much to establish.

I believe that I have come to understand anxiety so much better through living with my beautiful ten-year-old son, Benedict. He is a special gift. I will not go into details but anxiety has been a very deep challenge for him and for our whole family. For Benedict, one of the symptoms of anxiety can be an obsessive need to live in a controlled world. He always needs to know exactly what we are doing today. The rules of anything are extremely important to him. Life has to stick to a script.

Through Benedict, I have come to understand not only my own anxiety but also that of my other family, the Catholic community. Since I left school about 34 years ago, I have seen the Church move along the autism spectrum to the point of disorder: it has become overly concerned about control, following a rigid script and making sure that it meets the world only on its own terms. It can only deal with people if they are prepared to come onto its turf and play by its rules. It finds open-ended relationships almost impossible. Its need for answers prevents it from enjoying stories with all their layers. Its need for control has made possible the keeping of some dire secrets.

Nowhere is this soul-destroying anxiety more apparent to me than in attitudes to liturgy. The missal has recently been re-translated into the kind of English that nobody actually speaks: it is a fearful step away from reality and a retreat to a safe and controlled place. This is not what liturgy is about. One of my favourite phrases in the Mass used to be "protect us from all anxiety as we wait in joyful hope" and

I used to pray those words with all my heart. It is a shame that they have disappeared and, like so much else, been replaced by something made of plastic. Real prayer, of which liturgy is a huge part, always needs an element of untidiness because it is human beings who are reaching out to God and God who is reaching out to us, not computers engaged in some kind of interface. Prayer is about reality. I find it hard to believe that Jesus died on the cross, naked, so the rest of us could have a fancy dress party.

Nevertheless, I do understand why these things have happened and I feel compassion about that. Many people experience the world as nerve-wracking. It can be a terrifying place and numbers of people have sought refuge in a tightly defined Church. But building walls and hiding behind them is not going to help very much. It is great that Pope Francis is urging us to end the siege mentality. For Christians, there is no such thing as *them* and *us*. There is only *us*. I hope Pope Francis will underline the importance of humour in liturgy. Before he became pope, he said:

> I am sincerely convinced that, at the present time, the fundamental choice that the Church must make is not that of diminishing or taking away precepts, of making this or that easier, but of going into the street in search of the people, of knowing persons by name. And not only because going to proclaim the Gospel is its mission, but because if it does not do so it harms itself. It is obvious that if one goes into the street it can also happen that one has an accident, but I prefer a thousand times over an accident-ridden Church to a sick Church.

I will end with one last story. It comes from my belief that the way to disentangle ourselves from anxiety is at least partly to allow time and space and importance in our lives for things which have no pragmatic value, no dollar value and no status value. It matters enormously that we make room for what does not matter. I love the Latin language, for example. I tell the teenagers I teach that the reason to learn Latin is chiefly that there is no material reason to do so. We have good reason to do things which have no earthly reason.

My story reflects this. Some years ago, my wife, Jenny, and I were living in a small country town of about 500 residents. Gunning is halfway between Goulburn and Yass on what used to be the Hume Highway. We had three children under the age of three and ran out of money, so we packed up to return to Melbourne where a wonderful school had been foolish enough to offer me a job.

One day, I was filling boxes and Jenny took the kids down to the park where she happened to find a wallet. There was no money in it. But it did have an American Express gold card in the name of Count Alexei Schmidt. It also had a rent-payer's card from the housing commission of NSW, likewise made out to Count Alexei Schmidt. There could not have been too many wallets that housed both these cards. Finally, there was a membership card for the Russian Club, also made out to Count Alexei Schmidt. The thing about my wife is that she married a genius. After close examination and deep thought, I announced: "I think this wallet belongs to Count Alexei Schmidt."

To cut a long story short, a friend drew our attention to an article in *The Goulburn Post*. It turned out that Count Alexei Schmidt was at that moment pushing a shopping trolley along the Hume Highway from Sydney to Melbourne (or perhaps it was Wagga) dressed as Napoleon. A reporter asked him why he was doing this. "Well," replied the count, "it is something I have always wanted to do."

Perhaps pushing a shopping trolley along the Hume Highway dressed as Napoleon is an eccentric thing to do, but what an amazing aspiration to have carried through your life. The count was following a dream which was completely disentangled from the customary anxieties which shape our aspirations. Most of us push shopping trolleys as far as the car and then unload the contents into the fridge that hides behind our fridge magnets. But here was a man who seemed to have floated free, a man of Tolstoyan vision. He clearly was not making much out of the endeavour: we later re-united the count with his wallet in the Yass hospital where he was recovering from heat exhaustion.

We have mourned this year the passing of one of the great souls of our time, the Irish poet Seamus Heaney. Heaney stood up over and over again for the playfulness of language and the unpragmatic importance of poetry, things of beauty and truth whose calling was simply to exist. Heaney's last words to his wife, Marie, were apparently texted in Latin. He said "*noli timere*", "don't be afraid". He once wrote a poem for his wife which included this stanza:

> *Love, you shall perfect for me this child*
> *Whose small imperfect limits would keep breaking:*
> *Within new limits now, arrange the world*
> *Within our walls, within our golden ring.*

Mary MacKillop likewise calls us beyond our habits of fear.

11

Mission Shapes Identity

Andrew Hamilton SJ

I was delighted to be invited to attend and reflect on the Catholic Social Services Victoria conference on Identity and Mission. It offered an opportunity to meet people in different organisations for whom the connection between identity and mission is vital. As a theologian I also hoped for stimulation to reflect on the way in which mission and identity are related in Australian society today. Personally, too, it offered an occasion to call to mind how my own understanding has developed over thirty or so years.

In this reflection on the conference I shall begin by tracing my own journey of understanding, and then reflect on some of the features of the conference. I shall conclude by suggesting briefly how Pope Francis has simplified and encouraged the task we share.

For much of my life I took identity and mission for granted. I was a Jesuit, a member of a Catholic religious order that ran schools, parishes and other works. After all I was a Catholic and Jesuit and so were our schools and parishes. So nothing more needed be said about identity. Because our works were staffed by Jesuits with the help of a few dedicated lay people it could be taken for granted that they carried out their mission. The questions that we talked about concerned how best to do so.

My first significant personal discovery came through vacation work with Jesuit Refugee Service at the Cambodian border in the early 1980s. At first this involved a few Jesuits who were placed mainly within a Thai Catholic agency, one of many faith-based and secular agencies working in the refugee camps. I began then to ask what was distinctive about our work. I was not interested in what differentiated us from other agencies, usually a dead end question, but in what qualities must characterise our work if we were to carry out our mission.

I came to identify that quality with an adamantine focus on the good of the refugees in all that we did and in all the decisions we took, no matter what the cost to the organisation. This was based in the human dignity of each person, which demanded that we respect both refugees and our fellow workers. As a Catholic I grounded this focus in God's love for each human being shown in the Incarnation and death of Christ. But, of course, it was shared by many other agencies. They grounded it in different ways. In the ambiguous moral world of the border region, the implications of this focus were tested regularly.

I also began to ask how that sharply focused mission could be maintained and handed on to others. Jesuit Refugee Service grew quickly and was quickly joined by other religious and lay volunteers. In meetings, prayer and appeals to the Gospel had an accepted place in deciding what path to take. But as the demands of the work were growing, the number of younger Jesuits and religious available to undertake it diminished. I began to notice, too, that in Australia fewer religious were available to offer leadership in other Catholic social agencies.

I identified this challenge of passing on the mission essentially as one of leadership. Strong lay leaders committed through faith to unwavering respect for the dignity of the people their organisation served would preserve its ethos. I recognised that people working in secular agencies often trumped us in their commitment to the dignity of those they served. But I also noticed that in some initially faith-based groups that had become secularised the quality of their attention to human dignity had seemed to diminish. So strong leadership, both in faith and in service, was required to sustain it.

The solution I advocated then was that Catholic agencies should search out and prepare committed young people for leadership. Groups encouraging young adults to be concerned for social justice provided a natural resource.

This proposal, however, became increasingly implausible. The decline in the number of religious available to offer leadership and carry on the spirit of Catholic organisations was matched by a corresponding decline in the number of committed lay Catholics. As a result, it would be hard to find committed Catholics to fill positions in which particular skills and experience were required.

At the same time Catholic groups working with young adults were also in decline. The reasons for this included a lack of the young religious who had traditionally led the ministry, the alienation of many young Catholics over the growing scandal of sexual abuse and the treatment of women, and the economic forces leading students to spend more time in paid work. Of the young adult groups that flourished, most focused on devotion and consolidation of belief rather than on social outreach.

This change questioned my assumption that the earlier structure of organisations led by religious could be maintained by replacing the religious with a few well-trained lay leaders. The reality was that organisations were lay, and had to develop formation processes to integrate the faith on which they were based with the radical respect for human dignity embodied in their mission.

This movement to shaping a Catholic identity that was led by respect for the people whom we serve was in some tension with directions taken within the Catholic Church. The shaping of identity was seen through the lens of the demands of the inner life of the Church. Catholic identity was based on an ideal of Catholic life characterised by regular participation in Church activities, a way of life in conformity with Church teaching, and whole hearted acceptance of the Church teaching on faith and morality. It was also associated with a strong emphasis on the distinctive status of priests within Catholic theology and life.

This approach to identity naturally stressed the importance of Catholic organisations appearing to be Catholic, and so of Catholic symbols. Catholic identity was to be asserted, sometimes combatively, in the face of secular society. These trends caused some unease among people working in Catholic organisations whose attitudes to Catholicism were conflicted. They were exacerbated by regulations enforced in particular cases that would exclude laicised priests, people in irregular marital situations and people in gay relationships from teaching in Catholic schools. In this climate concern for identity could obscure the importance of mission.

Out of this experience I came to the conference with four questions:

- First, would I find foremost a focus on the dignity of the people whom the organisations serve, and the conviction that this focus on mission shapes questions of identity?
- Second, with what realism and enthusiasm were Catholic lay organisations nurturing mission and identity in a diverse staff?

- Third, how was the nurturing of identity and mission negotiated within a Catholic Church that sometimes saw identity to have to do primarily with intra-church relationships?
- And finally, what further questions would the conference raise?

The Conference

When reflecting on these questions during the conference I was encouraged by what I saw and heard. The participants were realistic and enthusiastic in the face of the task they had accepted.

They recognised clearly the difficulties caused by the hollowing out of so many Church bodies and institutions and by the current ills of the Church. They also grappled with the lack of Catholic formation in many of their Catholic staff, with the increasing number of staff members from other churches or religions, and with their lack of resources for sharing the spirit of their organisations.

The situation evoked for me the image of someone commissioned to bring water to a distant settlement, only to find that the dam from which the water came was leaking, the tankers in which it was brought were also leaking, as were the tanks in the settlements to which it was delivered. The drivers worked with great spirit, trying to patch their tankers on the run.

The image conveys some of the challenge in sharing identity and mission, and of the gallantry of those involved in it. They described their task in simple terms, avoiding the elevated theological language that smoothes out the difficulties and prematurely spiritualises the task.

I was also struck by the matter of fact and cheerful acceptance by most Catholic organisations that they are lay and are animated by laypeople. Few people saw demarcation disputes between laity and clergy or religious as a major problem, and the nurturing of mission identity was a priority within most organisations.

Those responsible for mission felt reasonably well supported in their task. The days, for example, when the religious education co-ordinator in a school would last six months and leave discouraged seem to have passed. Now the priority given to passing on the faith is often reflected in structures and processes. So in many schools the faith co-ordinators or heads of mission may be deputy heads. In health care and in many other ministries, too, the importance of mission is recognised in the organisational structure. This does not make the task easy, but it may make it possible.

In the formal conference program I found this note of encouragement and realism struck by the presentations of keynote speaker Chris Lowney and of Bishop Eugene Hurley, as well as by Michael McGirr in his dinner speech (Mary MacKillop Oration). Each in his own way acknowledged the reality of the world in which we work, the importance of good companions and the primacy of the mission to respect human dignity.

Evident at the conference was the easy acceptance of diversity of belief in Catholic organisations. Participants generally saw this as a challenge but not as an obstacle to introducing people to the connection between mission and its faith basis. They were not intimidated by the task. They accepted difference as a fact of life that was in many ways beneficial, and remained convinced that, in their own tradition and the stories that embodied it, they had a resource worth sharing.

They were also committed to being inclusive when presenting

the mission and identity of their organisation. They did not allow staff to feel that acceptance of faith was a condition of full or real membership, but allowed people to respond and own in their own way the language and symbols of mission. Diversity was a gift because it allowed people from a different background to illuminate and to help shape the mission.

Underlying people's ease in speaking of the identity of their organisation was their deep conviction that it existed for the people whom they served. People and their human dignity mattered most. Although conceptually and historically this mission may flow out of the identity and history of each organisation, in its actual life the mission comes first. Still, it remains essential to welcome staff into the stories and symbols of identity in order to nurture the mission.

The conference left me pondering some challenges and questions that organisations will face in coming years. The first concerns the tension between professionalism and the mission to people who are disadvantaged. From the point of view of the mission, the first call is to shape good relationships with the people we serve, to become companions. Those relationships are the engine of human development and discovery. The people best at building these relationships sometimes lack professional qualifications. The main gift of others will be their intuitive grasp of the relationship between the faith basis and the quality of service demanded by the mission.

But the mission to people also requires that we serve them as skillfully and sustainably as possible. That is why professional competence is required. The challenge is to see professionalism as a means to serving people effectively but not as an end in itself.

The balance between professionalism and mission also draws attention to the qualities we seek in Catholic organisations. They should include professional expertise, openness to the spirit of the organisation, and a natural gift for building the relationships so central within the mission.

Another challenge is to maintain our focus on respect for the human dignity of the people we serve when in so much of our work we are agents of government. We are reliant on government funding, must work within the demands for accountability governments place on us, and will constantly be faced with conditions that compromise aspects of our mission. For example, the current fashion of asking individuals to choose service modules privileges the benefits of individuals making economic choices. But for some individuals, whose circumstances and background make that kind of choice ineffectual, it may impede the development of the stable relationships needed to help them make reasonable choices.

The emphasis on efficiency, too, may lead governments to prefer large service providers. That, in turn, would lead to pressure for small Catholic organisations to form partnerships with large for-profit providers. They might then find it difficult to maintain in their work the respect for human dignity and the building of relationships that their mission demands.

Changes in relationship to governments driven by the need to make less funds cover more projects, of course, are not simply a threat. They are also an opportunity to re-imagine the needs that we meet and the ways we meet them. Indeed, the history of Catholic agencies is a tribute to the capacity for reinvention.

In his Mary MacKillop Oration, Michael McGirr's humorous but telling warning against the danger of anxiety, and his exhortation to boldness were salient. He was saddened by the inability of students focused on their VCE year to begin to imagine why someone might want to dress up as Napoleon and walk from Melbourne to Sydney while pushing a pram. Anxiety closes down the space the Catholic imagination needs to entertain the quixotic and inefficient.

If we are to respect the human dignity of the people with whom we work and to enlarge their imagination of what is possible, our own dreams need to be large and our imagination capable of conceiving the apparently odd. Anxiety is the enemy of the creative imagination.

The conversation at the conference was mostly free and bold. A large challenge in Catholic groups is to be bold in speaking the truth to authority. In my experience most conversations about the Catholic Church turn quickly to clerical sexual abuse and its effects, to the attitude to women and to abuses of authority. These things affect the morale of our staff and affect the welfare of those whom we serve. They compromise our mission. At the conference they were aired, but the airing seemed to be considered an extraordinary act of boldness rather than an ordinary conversation about mission. If that impression is right, anxiety and boldness should remain on the agenda.

Pope Francis and the Future

I shall conclude by reflecting on the way Pope Francis is shaping the Catholic approach to identity and mission. In his words and gestures he affirms the way in which the participants at the conference saw their work, and will encourage and simplify reflection on it.

Francis has placed our work at the centre of the Church by insisting that Catholics generally should go out from the comfortable centre of Church to people at its edges, and through our relationship to them to help them find God's compassion in their lives. He has put priority on the mission and allows it to shape our understanding of our identity.

Francis has also insisted that it should be part of Catholic identity to be inclusive. He does not judge people as different or expect them to enter the symbols of identity on his terms. We should also expect this openness to faith and inclusiveness from our staff. From this perspective, Catholic organisations are not defined by their difference from the non-Catholic world or secular world, but by the quality of their mission, by the experience of compassion on which it is built, and by their respect for difference.

The simplicity of Francis' vision highlights the hope on which Catholic mission rests. Even if the existing forms of government funding were to change so that no niche were left for publicly funded organisations, people who have experienced God's compassion will come together to care for the neglected. The impulse to love and to embody it in relationships that transform the lives of people who are disadvantaged will endure.

Finally, at a time when the Catholic Church was becoming locked into an internal language, the Pope has demonstrated the power of symbols. His symbols have mainly to do with mission and reaching out into the world outside the Church. People have been struck by his choosing to leave the conclave by bus rather than the papal limo,[93] by his going to a juvenile detention centre for Holy Thursday Mass and washing the feet of young men and women, Muslim as well as Christian,[94] and by his going to the asylum-seeker island of Lampedusa where his altar was made of the wood of broken-up boats.[95]

---

93 See ncronline.org/news/vatican/how-pope-francis-spent-his-first-24-hours-after-conclave – accessed on 15 January 2014.
94 See edition.cnn.com/2013/03/28/world/europe/vatican-pope – accessed on 15 January 2014.
95 See vatican.va/holy_father/francesco/homilies/2013/documents/papa-francesco_20130708_omelia-lampedusa_en.html, 8 July, 2013 – accessed on 15 January 2014.

The symbols of Catholic identity remain important: the crucifixes in school rooms and wards, the statues and paintings of founders and the icons of saints, and the connections with the Catholic Church in naming and through boards.

These symbols remind people of their mission. But the most important symbols will be those that enable those to whom we reach out to experience Christ's compassion. Some symbols, like crucifixes, do this naturally. But the others we make, and they will form the stories for future generations as have the symbols that Pope Francis has made.

12

Listening, Learning and Leading
– A Continuing Dialogue:
Inspiring Us to be Christ in the World Today

Denis Fitzgerald

Introduction

A conference brings people together around a theme, and it facilitates input by way of papers, workshops, discussion, etc. It gives participants time to reflect, and creates a variety of opportunities for discussion. A good conference, by its structure and the sequence of topics, creates an enriching dialogue among participants. It also equips participants with ideas, understanding, inspiration and contacts that can enable them to continue to develop, implement and share around the conference themes beyond the conference itself.

The conference from which the papers in this volume are drawn sought "to inspire, challenge and resource around mission-focused leadership, with an emphasis on practical implications for leaders and organisations".[96] Around 180 members and associates of Catholic Social Services Victoria took time in Melbourne on 9-10 October 2013 to listen and reflect and learn, and concluded that it was time well spent. In the words of one participant, a leading practitioner in their field:

> I enjoyed the conference ... interesting ... lots of good

---

96 Denis Fitzgerald, "Identity and Mission", *Kairos*, 2013, 24(7), p. 22; accessed on 6 February 2014 at cam.org.au/Kairos.

people ... energising commitment to the 'mission' ... honest about the challenges they suffer ... all in all, good stuff!

The chapters in this book give a good sense of the input that was provided over the two days of the conference. But the conference was much more than that, because that input was the starting point for significant dialogue and engagement that enlivened the gathering.

In seeking to communicate that dynamic of the conference, this chapter reflects on some of the themes that were common across a number of speakers, such as the Gospel roots of our calling, and the invitation this extends to us; and the advantages and challenges of the diverse religious environment that is the reality for many Catholic social service providers.

A significant part of this chapter is devoted to Bishop Eugene Hurley's closing address to the conference, which was entitled "Challenged and Inspired to be Christ in the World Today". Eugene Hurley is the Bishop of Darwin and chairman of the Australian Catholic Bishops' Commission for Pastoral Life. Bishop Eugene's call for faith-inspired engagement with the world neatly drew together the key themes of many of the other presenters. He drew heavily on his experience of working with Indigenous communities, asylum seekers and others. And out of these encounters with the beloved of Christ, Bishop Eugene called on all to strive, with love, to close the chasm between the Church and Christ; to heal the wounds, warm the hearts, and be close to the people, since "the blazing glory of the Resurrection far surpasses any human weaknesses and their effects".

Responding to the Gospel Call

The hope and the energy that Pope Francis has brought to the Church and the world was part of our narrative at this conference. He was referred to by nearly every speaker. Conference keynote speaker and visiting US author Chris Lowney's book[97] on Pope Francis and his leadership was launched during the conference.

But, as Pope Francis insists, our mission goes back to the Gospels – speaker after speaker reflected on the centrality of the Gospel mission to Catholic service: to love one another as Christ has loved us; to reach out to the least of our brothers and sisters; to reveal Christ to those whom we serve.

Love of neighbour, and loving service to those most in need, are integral to our relationship with Christ, as the Last Judgement passage in St Matthew's Gospel spells out. Here the King tells those assembled that in feeding the hungry, welcoming the stranger, visiting those imprisoned, and so on, they were serving him: "I tell you solemnly, in so far as you did this to one of the least of these brothers and sisters of mine, you did it to me." (*Matthew* 25: 40)

Each of us is called to live out this call, but it is also a responsibility of the Church collectively. As Pope Benedict XVI put it in his encyclical letter, *Deus Caritas Est* (*God is Love*): "The Church cannot neglect the service of charity any more than she can neglect the Sacraments and the Word."[98] And this work of charity is intimately connected with striving for social justice.

Catholic social service organisations work to further this social mission of the Gospel. Julie Edwards of Jesuit Social Services explained how the Gospel mission, as reflected in Catholic Social Teaching and the Ignatian tradition, pervades all aspects of their work. Chris Lowney outlined how a sense of purpose that is greater

---

97 Chris Lowney, *Pope Francis: Why He Leads the Way He Leads*, Loyola Press, Chicago, 2013; see chrislowney.com – accessed on 6 February 2014.
98 Pope Benedict XVI, Encyclical Letter, *Deus Caritas Est*, 2005, section 22; accessed on 6 February 2014 at vatican.va.

than the self and which pervades the work of Catholic social services is inherently spiritual.

Strength and Challenges in Diversity

Catholic social service organisations,[99] and the communities with which they work, are diverse in many ways: some are quite large, providing a range of services from dozens of locations, while others operate from just one site and are focused on a single service; some organisations operate across Victoria or other States, and beyond, but many are locally based; some services are part of parish structures, or sponsored by dioceses or religious congregations; others are more autonomous, reflecting many different historical settings. The services that are provided by the sector as a whole, ranging from aged care to youth support, seek to address most areas of human need, and these services are provided to the community as a whole.

Another dimension of diversity is in the faith commitment of staff within these organisations. Little hard data is available, but for some time now it has been clear that there have been increasing numbers of staff who identify with the values and the social mission of our organisations, but who are not Catholics.[100] This extends to leadership roles within some organisations, including, in some cases, Board membership.

This diversity both enriches and challenges Catholic social service

---

99 See the Catholic Social Services Victoria website for a listing of the approximately 50 member organisations and of the services that are provided: css.org.au – accessed on 6 February 2014. The website of Catholic Social Services Australia lists its 60 member organisations: cssa.org.au – accessed on 6 February 2014.
100 See, for example, Frank Quinlan, "Common Challenges for Health, Education and Social Services" in Neil Omerod (ed.), *Identity and Mission in Catholic Agencies*, St Pauls Publications, Strathfield, 2008, pp. 39-58.

providers. As Julie Edwards put it: "We have a treasure – a bunch of good people doing good things, within an invitational, Catholic setting".

The diversity enriches our organisations in many ways, including by bringing a range of skills, insight and commitment to which we would not otherwise have access – larger organisations would be very hard pressed to operate without these staff. In quite a number of cases, leadership by people who are not Catholic but committed to the Catholic identity and mission of Catholic social service providers has been invaluable. The Church, and the community that we serve, is indebted to them.

But there are challenges that flow from this too. How do we articulate a religious vision in a diverse environment? How do we gain commitment to a vision that is grounded in concepts and beliefs that are not shared throughout the organisation?

Margaret Mary Flynn ibvm was one of the speakers who shared insights on this: the mission statement at CentaCare Wilcannia Forbes provided a sense of corporate identity through its pivotal role in recruitment and induction; through staff reflection on it; and in its use as a tool for discernment. Engagement in this was open to all staff.

Leading all staff to reflect on their spiritual well-spring was seen as an integral part of this. As several of the papers note, people join organisations for a reason, because of a belief in the work that is being done, and we all respond positively to interest in our own perspectives!

Many speakers and commentators noted that staff generally embraced enthusiastically the principles and the application of Catholic Social Teaching, which provides a common language for much reflection and discernment. And it is a responsibility of the organisation as a whole to give staff that opportunity to engage, for it is they who will build the mission in reality. As CatholicCare Melbourne chief executive officer Fr Joe Caddy put it in one discussion: the call to engagement with staff in humility and mission is a call to conversion for all of us.

"Formation of the Heart" in a Diverse Faith Environment

As Catholic Social Teaching can be a very positive point of entry to the mission of a Catholic agency, so too can it engage all staff in reflection on how things are done. For example, Pope Benedict XVI in *Deus Caritas Est* identified as key features of Catholic social services humility in our engagement with others and a spirit of dialogue with the world.[101] These two themes, each developed by speakers at the conference, resonate easily among people of good will, and are areas where the Church has much to learn from others.

But some features of a Catholic identity can be more challenging for a diverse organisation to embrace. Everyone – whether or not they be Catholic, Christian or people of faith – is challenged particularly by Pope Benedict's reflection on the ministry of service and of work for justice:

> Consequently, in addition to their necessary professional training, these charity workers need a "formation of the heart": they need to be led to that encounter with God in Christ which awakens their love and opens their spirits to others. As a result, love of neighbour will no longer be for them a commandment imposed, so to speak, from without, but a consequence deriving from their faith, a faith which becomes active through love.[102]

---

101 Pope Benedict XVI, op. cit., sections 34-35.
102 Ibid., section 31.

At the conference, Barry Sheehan from CatholicCare Toowoomba and Patricia McCourt from the St Vincent de Paul Society, in responses to Margaret Mary Flynn's presentation, highlighted the importance of leaders' positive engagement with the specifically Christian dimensions of the organisation, and sharing with staff and stakeholders of diverse backgrounds their vision of engagement with the "face of God". Chris Lowney on several occasions placed personal spirituality at the heart of personal effectiveness, and thus reflection on this as part of the leadership role of each person. Shared prayer, community Mass, etc., can be equally as challenging for such staff, for they too are, as for the general society, countercultural.

Within our organisations, a dialogue on these challenging dimensions of mission and identity is a necessary part of making the mission a shared, living reality. Only within such a dialogue – across the whole organisation – can these issues of formation be effectively advanced, and dialogue around the nature and direction of our services and the identity of our organisations be sufficiently robust.

"Preach the Gospel always, when necessary use words" is an insight attributed to St Francis of Assisi, and is one that leaders work with often in this area. This is a necessary step – for unless what we do and how we lead is aligned with the Gospel, words about these matters are unlikely to be effective.

And the dialogue around issues of identity and mission that can flow from consideration of Catholic Social Teaching and the impact of mission on our work can often be a starting point for dialogue on why and how we do it.

But such dialogue is not easy. It is constrained by time, expertise and method, to name just a few aspects. It can be more complex in a diverse faith environment. The conference resourced participants to advance this dialogue in a complex environment, and the papers in this volume encapsulate much of that resource.

As a society, we are not good at discussing matters of religion, so one temptation is to strip the principles of their religious heritage and connection. But that would be to risk cutting the organisation adrift from its roots. Julie Edwards' narrative of the tree with deep, nourishing roots resounded with conference participants, as it does with her colleagues at Jesuit Social Services. The conference as a whole was a helpful stage for many in empowering them to advance personally in this journey within their organisations.

The bottom line is that we can only carry out our mission as organisations in community. As Chris Lowney put it in his concluding remarks, "It absolutely makes a difference when our people buy the mission" – that is our challenge. "This is the team the Holy Spirit has put on the playing field", he reflected, and so it is this team that we need to know and lead. As Fr Andrew Hamilton SJ added, one of the ways in which our faith needs to show itself is in our respect for those who do not share it.

And the dialogue can only be sustained by a supportive community, within our organisations and beyond. To build a vibrant mission-oriented organisation, we need continually to reflect on our life and work, and seek to understand our mission. We need to communicate this understanding through a narrative that is woven through our endeavours. We need to live the mission, in dialogue with the world, and we need continually to tell our story. In doing so, we build a community of shared commitment that will sustain the mission over time.[103]

---

[103] For further development of these points, see Denis Fitzgerald, "Grounding our Mission in a Story", presentation to the Australasian Catholic Press Association, 5 September 2013; accessed on 6 February 2013 at css.org.au.

Many organisations work to build such a community, and support is available within the Catholic social services' community. The continued development of this framework within which the mission of the Gospel can flourish in individual organisations remains a priority for the sector.

Challenged and Inspired to be Christ in the World Today

Bishop Eugene Hurley of Darwin celebrated Mass as part of the conference, and delivered the final keynote address entitled "Challenged and Inspired to be Christ in the World Today".

Bishop Eugene adopted as a framework for his address the importance of our vision of the Church, of Jesus Christ and of the world: "If we don't get our vision of those three things right, then we're in a bit of bother". For, following the American Jesuit psychologist John Powell, the way we envision a person, event, situation, etc., will play a large part in determining our response to it.[104]

Bishop Eugene identified this alignment of vision as a key challenge to the Church today: he had been "amazed and depressed" by focus group research from the US that found that when people were asked to respond spontaneously to the term 'Jesus', they responded with things like "compassionate", "cares for the poor", "forgiving of sinners", "loving". But when asked to respond to the word 'Church', they responded with a different set of words: "irrelevant", "negative", "out of touch", "powerful", "lacking in understanding of ordinary people's lives".

He continued with a story of a dying man who had been estranged from the Church since his parish priest had told him that he could not bury the man's son, who had committed suicide:

---

104 See, for example, John Powell and Michael H. Cheney, *A Life-Giving Vision: How to Be a Christian in Today's World*, Thomas More Association, Allen TX, 1995.

And I stood there thinking to myself this is a shame, and I made an awful mistake. I said to him, "Look I'm so sorry that this terrible incident has separated you from God all this time", and he nearly spat at me. He said: "It never separated me from God, only the Church". And I thought to myself, when we have a situation where somebody can separate God and the Church that Jesus Christ instituted something's gone very, very wrong! Because they should overlay one another perfectly.

Bishop Eugene told how, on behalf of the Church, he had asked the man's forgiveness:

And so I said to him: "Look, I can't help that, I can't make it right again, it was never right, it wasn't right then, it's not right now, it never will be right. The only thing I can do is ask for your forgiveness, and you can tell me to nick off or you can forgive the Church, but that's your business".

So I knelt down and said: "I ask you now on behalf of the Church that has offended you in this way, would you please forgive us?" It took him a while, and he eventually grunted, "I suppose so", which was good enough for me. So I stood up and thanked him. I said: "Now I'm your priest and I'm going to give you absolution" and so I did. I said, "I'd like to go and get you communion". He said: "I'd love that".

Bishop Eugene then linked this story, and that of "the many other good people who love God and love the Church but who are alienated from the Church" to the challenges and inspiration of trying to be Christ in the world – such people are so inspiring, and the challenge is to prevent this alienation!

He noted that, taking a different approach, Pope Francis is challenging us in a new and practical way, and has stressed a different aspect of the Church in the following words:

I see clearly that the thing the Church most needs today is the ability to heal the wounds and to warm the hearts of the faithful; it needs nearness, proximity. I see the Church as a field hospital after battle. It is useless to ask a seriously injured person if he has high cholesterol and about the level of his blood sugars! You have to heal his wounds. Then we can talk about everything else. Heal the wounds, heal the wounds ... And you have to start from the ground up. The Church sometimes has locked itself up in small things, in small-minded rules. The most important thing is the first proclamation: Jesus Christ has saved you.[105]

Bishop Eugene effectively communicated the strength with which this resonated with him:

What a vision of the Church! Now that's why the man is so happy, why he's out and about, why he's engaging with people, because his emotional response to that vision of the Church demands that he be out and about, that he be close to people, listen to people, go to Lampedusa because there are people there that are dying at sea.

Bishop Eugene identified further challenges for Australian Catholics in responding to this formulation of the Gospel calling. One is "the risk of being seduced into being like all other successful people":

It's a good time for us as the Catholic community to ask ourselves questions, lest we drift thoughtlessly from a special place to some other seemingly more successful place.

He linked this challenge to that faced by Aboriginal communities

---

[105] Pope Francis, quoted in Antonio Spadaro, "A Big Heart Open to God", *America: The National Catholic Review*, 30 September 2013; accessed on 6 February 2014 at americamagazine.org.

that form part of his people in the Northern Territory, communities that "in so many ways [have] become what they've admired and in doing so I think in many ways they've lost what was precious. They're drunk and violent and sophisticated in the ways of the world like the rest of us".

But this is not that to which they aspire. Bishop Eugene continued:

> I have had and still have the pleasure and the privilege of sitting with lots of our Indigenous leaders, and one of the most extraordinary times for me was sitting with people at Wadeye – which is quite a big Aboriginal community of my diocese of about 4,000 people – and I said: "I'm your Bishop. You know I will oppose anything you want me to oppose, I'll promote whatever you want me to promote, and I'll say nothing about what you want me to say nothing about, but I don't know what these matters are."
>
> So they spoke in Murrinhpatha, which is their language, for quite a long time and eventually they said to me: "Bishop, this is it: these are things you must always remember about us. The first thing you must remember is that we are a Catholic community. Secondly, Bishop, that is not 'what we are' it is 'who we are'".

Bishop Eugene then reflected that he had been "saddened and disturbed to see a very different culture swirling around their communities as very successful, powerful people intruded into their lives without consultation and imposed solutions that take no account of who those people are". The "intervention people", for example, were not interested in speaking to Church personnel – "that was all that religious stuff; they were here to fix things up". They dismissed essential elements of the people's vision. It is obvious why the intervention does not work!

So too with the general Catholic community – it is:

It's so easy for us to slip out of the sacred into the more successful. And I ask the question: are we in the throes of achieving what we've always coveted and at the same time losing our identity as we forget our past and the paths of sacrifice by which we've travelled and the truths of faith that make us who we are?

In our achievement of success have we forgotten why we strove to have equal access to power and influence? Are we as truly committed to social justice as we were when we were a community clearly discriminated against? Or are we losing the authority to speak on the plight of the poor? Are we now 'the other'? ... If we're not different then presumably we're the same as everybody else, as every other agency, as every other NGO [non-government organisation], as every other school. If we are the same, why are we in it? If we're not the same, what are the differences? And this is the challenge for me, because when I talk to the executive in our schools and CatholicCare, etc., I say: "Look our schools have got to be very, very, very good; I think they should be better than other schools, because people pay money to go there and make a deliberate decision to send their kids there. They should be better than other schools, but they should be very, very, very good Catholic schools. Tell me what makes them Catholic, not just very, very, very good schools. Our CatholicCare, what makes it Catholic?"

And we've got to come back, I think, to that vision that dictates what we 'get high' about, which is the mind and the heart and the touch and the voice of Jesus Christ. And that's what Pope Francis has said, if you want to know about the poor, you've got to go and touch them ...

> You've got to go and touch them without being too pious, because that's where Jesus lives. That's where he lives, and we need as a Church to have the hands and mind and heart of Jesus Christ, and I think it's no mystery that when we start doing that, that's very attractive to people because all of us need love like we need the air to breathe and I think that's what's captivated the world with Pope Francis, that he's a man that acts out of that.

Bishop Eugene developed the same themes from another perspective through reflection on his engagement over the years with people seeking asylum in Australia. A key point here, he emphasised, is human contact:

> I am so embarrassed that [in the 2013 federal election campaign] both major parties of our country gave no choice to us to indicate our basic compassion for people in need, and I have seen too many and I know the stories too well, to believe that, if we knew the stories, as an Australian community, we would countenance the morally bankrupt policies of both major parties ... once you keep them isolated so no-one can see them, then you can put a label on them and once you put the label on them you can treat them very differently. Our emotional response is to say well, to hell with them, they don't deserve to come here, so turn their boats around, get rid of them, because they're all flea-infested, queue jumpers – all these things that we don't like. And our emotional response is: get rid of them. ... And I just suggest it to you as a challenge to me and to you that, in a country like ours, it seems in fact to be a vote winner to be more brutal with people in need than the other party would be. This is a real challenge to the Australian culture, the Australian psyche, as to who we are, and I must say I feel

enormously embarrassed to be an Australian, that our two major political parties would have vied with each other to be more brutal than the other and found that to be an absolute vote winner.

Bishop Eugene drew powerfully on his own contact with refugees on Christmas Island, in Darwin and beyond, and what he had learnt from that. This reinforced the general point:

> When a boat had come into the Geraldton harbour, in the local paper, a fellow said, "I was always against these bloody refugees until I saw them", and he saw the boat come in and there they really were, the live men and women and children, all of a sudden his vision was different. But he'd never seen them before, because that's the arrangement; keep them out of sight because they've got no right to be here, no right to our compassion.

Bishop Eugene concluded with two inspiring ways of looking at Christ and the Church in the world.

The first was from Fr Stephen Rossetti, an American priest, who spoke some years ago about a "Resurrection vision". Bishop Eugene quoted from him:

> A Resurrection vision gives rise to a natural Christian optimism. Not a pollyannaish optimism that fails to recognize the ongoing devastation of sin and the reality of human suffering. But rather it is a strong optimism that recognizes that no matter how bad the devastation ... pedophilia, priest shortages, AIDS and the like ... these are far surpassed by the blazing glory of the Resurrection.[106]

---

106 Stephen J. Rossetti, *Origins*, 22 March 2001, 30(40), p. 643; accessed on 6 February 2014 at originsonline.com.

And the final inspiration was from Pope John Paul II, in the document that launched the Jubilee Year of 2000, where he wrote: "The Church is in the world as the living presence of the love of God who leans down to every human weakness in order to gather it into the embrace of his mercy".[107]

Bishop Eugene commented:

> What a beautiful vision of the Church! The Church is in the world, not hermetically sealed off somewhere from the 'naughty people' – the Church is in the world as the living presence of God! What a lovely thing to say! The Church is in the world as the living presence of the love of God, reaching down to every human weakness in order to gather it into his merciful embrace. What a beautiful, exciting, challenging, energising vision of the Church! ... it really is a graced-filled vision of the Church, it's really what we're about ... accept and embrace that and let all the other stuff fit neatly into that in its own time.

There was a rousing ovation, the strongest for the conference. The engagement of hearts and minds was palpable.

---

[107] Pope John Paul II, *Incarnationis Mysterium*, 1998, section 9; accessed on 6 February 2014 at vatican.va.

Contributor Details

DAVID BEAVER has been the Executive Director of Centacare Ballarat since October 1993, and has led an incredible period of growth seeing Centacare expand from seven staff to almost 200 and helping over 10,000 clients throughout half of Victoria. Prior to his current appointment, David worked with Centacare Melbourne from 1991 after ten years with St Vincent's Boys Home, mostly as Executive Director. David has years of experience in the community welfare, mental health and education sectors. He is a qualified social worker and a registered psychologist and also has business studies qualifications. Centacare's growth in the areas of relationship, family, psychiatric illness, homelessness and unemployment services can be directly attributed to David's expertise, business acumen, compassion and understanding of the needs of the disadvantaged in the community.

FRANK BRENNAN SJ AO is a Jesuit priest, human rights lawyer and academic who has made a significant contribution to Australian society as an advocate for justice and for reconciliation. Through service, publications and public engagement he has developed the Australian community's understanding of many dimensions of social justice and human rights, and has advanced the interests of Indigenous Australians, asylum seekers and many others. His Order of Australia citation reads: In recognition of service to Aboriginal Australians, particularly as an advocate in the areas of law, social justice and reconciliation. In 2009, Fr Brennan chaired the National Human Rights Consultation for the Australian Government. His current appointments include Professor of Law at the Australian Catholic University, and a Board member of St Vincent's Health Australia.

VICKI CLARK, Aboriginal woman living in the urban setting of Melbourne, is a Mutthi Mutthi woman inextricably linked to her country of Lake Mungo National Park in south-western NSW. Vicki has worked for 23 years as Co-ordinator at Aboriginal Catholic Ministry for Victoria, maintaining a centre that is a place of welcome and spiritual healing and at the same time working strongly as an advocate for justice for her people within the Catholic Church and the wider community. In 1994, Vicki was acknowledged by Victoria's *Herald Sun* newspaper in their list of "Great Victorians" for her leadership and service to the community and in 1998 won the Philia Award for Individual Initiative in this field. On Australia Day in 1999, the City of Darebin recognised her work for "Reconciliation through Education" with a Community Event Award. In May 2001, she was listed on the Centenary of Federation Honour Roll of "Women Shaping the Nation".

ROBERT DIXON is Director of the Pastoral Research Office of the Australian Catholic Bishops Conference. He has a Doctor of Philosophy from Monash University as well as degrees in science, theology and education. He is the author of *The Catholic Community in Australia* (2005) and co-author of several books and reports including *Catholics who have stopped attending Mass* (2007) and *Woman and Man: One in Christ Jesus – Report on the Participation of Women in the Catholic Church in Australia* (1999). Before becoming a social researcher, Bob taught mathematics, physics and religious education and was involved in school administration at several Catholic secondary schools in Melbourne and Western Samoa. He is an Adjunct Professor at the Australian Catholic University and a member of the Boards of the Christian Research Association and of NCLS Research.

JULIE EDWARDS has been Chief Executive Officer of Jesuit Social Services since June 2004, after joining the organisation in 2001. A social worker, family therapist and grief and loss counsellor, she has over 35 years experience engaging with marginalised people and families experiencing breakdown and trauma. Julie has a Master of Social Work degree and is currently completing her doctorate in this discipline. In January 2010, Julie became a Graduate of the Australian Institute of Company Directors. A Council member of Catholic Social Services Victoria, Julie also serves on a number of government committees that work to promote a more just society and contribute to the health and wellbeing of members of our community. Further, she is a member of the International Working Group on Death, Dying and Bereavement as well as a member of a number of national and international Jesuit commissions and working groups across the areas of justice, education, social ministry, governance of natural and mineral resources, and ecology. She is passionate about finding ways to give practical expression to her social justice values, exploring the most effective means to build a more just society, and promoting a values-based model of leadership.

DENIS FITZGERALD is Executive Director of Catholic Social Services Victoria (CSSV), the peak body for about 50 Catholic social services organisations. He has been in that role since March 2008. Denis' academic qualifications are in philosophy, accounting and public policy. His career has included work in international relations, public policy, and the delivery of Government services, and his Australian diplomatic roles service in High Commissions in London and the Solomon Islands, and with the World Bank in Washington DC. He served three years as Australia's High Commissioner to Nauru. Denis advised the Victorian Government on taxation, and on consumer protection, and administered a number of programs in these areas. For two years prior to his current role, Denis was Director, Corporate Services at CatholicCare Melbourne. At CSSV Denis works with its members in public policy, advocacy, strengthening cooperation within the sector, and reflecting with members on Catholic identity and its implications. He chairs the Victorian Council of Churches Social Questions Commission, and Interchurch Criminal Justice Taskforce, and is a member of a range of Government and advisory forums, including the Victoria Police Interfaith Advisory Council. Denis chaired the Steering Committee for the CSSV conference *Listening, Learning and Leading: The impact of Catholic identity and mission on what we do and how we do it.*

THE HON. TIMOTHY FISCHER AC was born at Lockhart, NSW, and educated at Boree Creek in the Riverina and Xavier College, Melbourne. He served with the Australian Army 1 RAR from 1966-1969, in both Australia and Vietnam, before returning to the family farm at Boree Creek. In 1971 he was elected to the NSW Parliament, where he became National Party Whip and served on a number of Parliamentary Committees. He resigned from State Politics in 1984 to seek pre-selection for the Federal Parliament and was subsequently elected Federal Member for Farrer, serving in this role from 1984-2001. During this time he was Shadow Minister for Energy and Resources, Shadow Minister for Trade, Leader of the National Party, and later Minister for Trade and Deputy Prime Minister in the Howard Government (1996-1999). He led the official delegation to observe the East Timor Referendum in 1999. Upon retiring from politics in 2001, he served as Chair of Tourism Australia (2004-2007) and then the first Rome-resident Australian Ambassador to the Holy See (2009-2012). He was also appointed by the Australian Government as

Special Envoy to Bhutan, Eritrea and South Sudan. In his work and related roles, he has visited over 84 countries. Mr Fischer has had a range of business interests and held numerous honorary positions. He is also a successful author. He lives at "Grossotto", Mudgegonga, Victoria, with his wife Judy and two sons, Harrison and Dominic, and at times at Boree Creek.

MARGARET MARY FLYNN ibvm completed her Arts degree and Diploma in Education before joining the Loreto Sisters. She has since completed further degrees in Counselling and Theology and is an alumna of the Stanford Graduate School of Business Executive Program for Nonprofit Leaders. Following a number of years teaching at Loreto Normanhurst and Toorak, and as Principal of Loreto Dawson Street, Ballarat, Margaret Mary worked in Melbourne as a family counsellor both within CentaCare and private practice. In 1996, she was asked to move to western NSW to develop a CentaCare agency on behalf of the Diocese of Wilcannia-Forbes, which covers the western 52 per cent of NSW. On her appointment as Loreto Province Leader in 2011, she moved to Melbourne from the bush, having built a substantial organisation with 31 branches and over 140 staff (25 per cent Indigenous) serving rural and remote communities throughout western NSW. Inspired by Mary Ward, Margaret Mary vigorously champions the rights of women and Indigenous communities and in 2010 won a NSW Telstra Business Women's Award in recognition of her work.

JENNY GLARE BBSc (La Trobe), BSW (Melbourne) has practised as a social worker since 1979. She has been employed by local, state and federal government departments and the not-for-profit sector as a caseworker, manager and consultant in the areas of child protection, family support and student assistance. Since the formation of MacKillop Family Services in July 1997, Jenny has led the development of the Heritage and Information Service and is responsible for the oversight and management of historical records and a support service for former residents of the founding agencies of MacKillop Family Services. The Heritage and Information Service has been recognised as an exemplar of best practice in the area of supported release of records to "Forgotten Australians". Jenny is currently a member of the Catholic Ethos and Identity Committee of Catholic Social Services Victoria.

ANDY HAMILTON SJ is a Jesuit priest. He is currently consulting editor of *Eureka Street* and works in the media department of Jesuit Social Services. He has contributed extensively to the publications *Eureka Street* and *Australian Catholics*, producing a steady stream of analysis of society and current issues from the perspective of a faith that demands work for justice. Andy has long been engaged with refugee communities and issues. He has served for many years as Chaplain to the Melbourne Laotian and Cambodian Catholic communities, and has written widely on refugee issues. Andy recently retired from a career of teaching Systematic Theology and Church History at the Melbourne College of Divinity.

PETER HUDSON is currently Network and Member Support Coordinator at Catholic Social Services Victoria. He is a former member of the Christian Brothers Oceania Province – he was one of the pioneering mission community sent to Tanzania in 1988 and ministered in various roles in East Africa for over a decade. Peter has extensive experience in cross-cultural living and religious formation. He holds degrees in Education, Arts and Business Studies and is a qualified and practising spiritual director.

CHRIS LOWNEY, formerly a Jesuit seminarian, later served as a Managing Director of JP Morgan & Co. in New York, Tokyo, Singapore and London until leaving the firm in 2001. He currently serves as chair of the board of Catholic Health Initiatives, one of the ten largest healthcare systems in the United States, comprising more than 70 hospitals in 19 states. His first book, *Heroic Leadership: Best Practices from a 450-Year-Old Company that Changed the World*, was the number 1-ranked bestseller of the Catholic Book Publishers Association and was named a finalist for a 2003 Book of the Year Award from *ForeWord* magazine. It has been translated into eleven languages. He is also author of *Heroic Living: Discover Your Purpose and Change the World* and *A Vanished World: Muslims, Christians, and Jews in Medieval Spain*, which was nominated for the *La corónica* Book Award. Chris was featured in the Public Broadcasting Service-aired documentary, *Cities of Light*, which echoed many of the book's key themes. He also helped launch Jesuit Commons: Higher Education at the Margins, which offers online-enabled university education in refugee camps; and the Ignatian Camino (caminoignaciano.org), a pilgrim trail tracking St Ignatius of Loyola's 1522 journey to Manresa. He is a *summa cum laude* graduate of Fordham University, where he also received his MA. He is holder of five honorary doctoral degrees.

MICHAEL MCGIRR is the Dean of Faith and Mission at St Kevin's College in Melbourne. He is the author of a number of books including *Things You Get for Free*, *Bypass: The story of a road* (currently a

VCE English text), *The Lost Art of Sleep* and *Finding God's Traces*. He has reviewed over 900 books for *The Age* and *The Sydney Morning Herald*. He loves singing Christmas carols at any time of year, a habit that appals both his wife, Jenny, and their three children. He is only allowed to sing in the garden but this may stop if the neighbours complain. He relishes the robust and pragmatic spirituality of teenagers. His students endure his weak jokes with admirable selflessness.

GABRIELLE MCMULLEN AM FRACI, BSc(Hons), PhD (Monash) is Emeritus Professor of Australian Catholic University (ACU). Following postdoctoral research in Germany she joined Monash University and also became Dean of its Catholic residence, Mannix College, in 1981. She was then Rector of ACU's Ballarat campus from 1995-2000 and its Pro- and Deputy Vice-Chancellor (Academic) until February 2011. She has a long-standing interest in the identity and mission of Catholic agencies and chaired ACU's Identity and Mission Committee for over a decade and convened the four cross-sectoral colloquia on identity and mission in Church-based organisations hosted by ACU in 2007-2010. Her community contributions have encompassed membership of education, health, theological and welfare boards. In July 2011, she was appointed a Trustee of Mary Aikenhead Ministries, which has been established by the Sisters of Charity of Australia to continue their health and aged care, education and welfare ministries.

JULIE MORGAN is a member of the Executive Education team at Australian Catholic University (ACU) and teaches within the Faculty of Theology and Philosophy's postgraduate leadership programs. Prior to joining ACU, Julie was employed in the health sector as Group Manager Social Justice – Policy and Practice at St Vincent's

Health Australia. She has worked previously as a management consultant to the not-for-profit sector and lecturer in Theology and Ethics at the Broken Bay Institute, where she also served on the Council. Julie has worked extensively throughout South-East Asia in the delivery of development and advocacy programming and in leadership development, human rights education and peacebuilding training. Her executive leadership experience includes working as the Deputy National Director of Caritas Australia and the Regional Director of Asia Pacific for Franciscans International. She has written extensively in the areas of peacebuilding, scripture and social justice for Australian and international publications. In 2002, Julie's work in international peacebuilding was formally recognised by the Prime Minister in an AusAID Citation.

JOHN WARHURST AO, who is Emeritus Professor of Political Science at the Australian National University, was born and bred in Adelaide and awarded his Doctor of Philosophy from the Flinders University of South Australia. He has published widely on religion and politics and also writes for *The Canberra Times* and *Eureka Street* magazine. John was formerly deputy chair of Catholic Social Services Australia and a member of the Australian Catholic Social Justice Council. He has authored three papers in the Catholic Social Justice series, including, most recently, *Charity and Justice: St Mary MacKillop and Australian Society*.

www.ingramcontent.com/pod-product-compliance
Lightning Source LLC
Chambersburg PA
CBHW070824250426
43671CB00036B/2067